Twenty-Five
Lessons in
CITIZENSHIP

Former Citiz

ISBN 1-879773-06-6
Library of Congress Control Number:2004107544
D.L. Hennessey Publishing
P.O. Box 115
Los Altos, CA 94023
Phone: (800) 355-5129
Fax: (800) 355-5129
E-mail: info@dlhpublishing.com
Website: www.dlhpublishing.com

Contents

Appendixes

In memory of
Lenore Richardson
and
Joan Richardson

Twenty-Five Lessons in Citizenship offers clear, concise, and accurate information about United States history and the make-up of national, state, county, and city governments for people who are studying to become citizens of the United States.

There has been a notable increase in the number of legal immigrants who are eligible for citizenship. Millions of people are either currently or soon to be eligible to naturalize in the United States. At the same time, the percentage of eligible candidates who actually naturalize has also risen. This rise will place a high demand on valuable resources like *Twenty-Five Lessons in Citizenship*.

In 2002, the United States Citizenship and Immigration Services (USCIS) replaced the Immigration and Naturalization Services (INS). *Twenty-Five Lessons in Citizenship* reflects this governmental shift.

For over seventy-five years, D.L. Hennessey's *Twenty-Five Lessons in Citizenship* has helped hundreds of thousands of people gain the historical, social and political background necessary to pass the citizenship exam. This book is a useful tool for individuals, immigration lawyers, adult education centers, English as a Second Language (ESL) courses, libraries, community colleges, and schools seeking to provide basic United States history and civics lessons to students.

D.L. Hennessey taught citizenship classes throughout Northern California. Erin Eriksson and Bryan Jones both hold Bachelor of Arts degrees in Political Science with concentrations in American Politics from the University of California, Los Angeles (UCLA). Bryan Jones also volunteers in citizenship classes taught in San Diego, California.

Introduction to Citizenship

About Twenty-Five Lessons in Citizenship

Congratulations on your decision to become a citizen of the United States. This book is appropriate for those who have already filed Form N-400, "Application to File Petition for Naturalization," which is the form used to apply to become a naturalized citizen. It is also for those who are just looking into becoming United States citizens. Regardless of where you are in the process, at some point you will have to complete the citizenship examination.

Twenty-Five Lessons in Citizenship offers clear, concise, and accurate information about United States history and the make-up of national, state, county, and city governments for people who are studying to become citizens of the United States. The citizenship examination will test your knowledge of United States history and government. This book includes the history and civics lessons to prepare you for the exam. In addition to testing your history and civics knowledge, your examiner will also test your ability to read, write, and speak English, as well as determine whether you have "good moral character." We recommend that you look at Appendix B and C for more information regarding English proficiency and good moral character.

As you continue the naturalization process, you will learn more about American civics, history, government, and politics, and will gain a richer understanding of the United States and its citizens.

How to Use this Book

We suggest that you go through each lesson in order. Pay particular attention to the questions at the end of each lesson. The questions listed under "USCIS 100 Sample Questions" are taken directly from the United States Citizenship and Immigration Services (formerly the Immigration and Naturalization Service) list of 100 sample questions. While the actual questions on your test may vary, you can expect to receive some of these questions from the sample set on the test. We have also included questions "For Further Study." These are questions that we have added to further test your understanding of the material. Answers to both sets of questions are included.

Information in this book is current as of the publication date. Although this book is updated frequently, you should pay attention to changing laws and policies. Additionally, references are made to political leaders who change often as new officers are elected. Please substitute current information as necessary.

Benefits of Citizenship

You have reasons for wanting to become a citizen of the United States, but let's review some of the benefits of American citizenship. We can divide the benefits of citizenship into two main groups: rights and responsibilities.

Rights

All people in the United States have rights; however, some are only specifically granted to citizens. As a citizen of the United States, you have the following rights as guaranteed in our Constitution and laws:

- **The right to vote:** As a citizen, you will be able to voice your opinions and make changes to the government by voting for your leaders. The right to vote is the most important right granted to United States citizens. This right also includes the right to join a political party of your choice and vote to promote your interests in free and fair elections.

- **The right to hold certain jobs:** Employment in certain jobs, especially those affiliated with the national government, may require American citizenship.

- **The right to travel with an American passport:** United States citizenship permits travel internationally with an American passport. Being an American citizen allows you some special rights and protections when traveling or living outside of the United States. Citizens may also return easily to the country.

- **The right to sponsor family members:** As a citizen, you may bring family—including parents, spouses, siblings, and children—into the country more quickly.

- **The right to live in the United States without restriction:** Once you are a citizen, you are no longer subject to scrutiny as a legal alien or resident. Anti-immigrant and deportation policies do not apply to citizens. Also, you will not have to carry a green card to prove that you are a legal alien.

- **The right to hold public office:** Naturalized citizens may run for and hold elected public office positions, except those of President and Vice-President.

- **The right to certain public social benefits:** Citizens have access to many public opportunities and benefits, including access to public education, scholarships and grants, Social Security, and welfare.

Responsibilities

Becoming a citizen also carries some responsibilities. To enjoy the freedoms and liberties that the Constitution and laws guarantee, as a citizen, you must follow your duties as an American to keep the nation running smoothly. Below is a list of responsibilities:

- **Voting:** Just as the freedom to vote is a right, it is also a responsibility. You must express your opinions by electing leaders that will make positive decisions.

- **Staying current with political events and affairs:** It is also important that you know current events so that you can make educated decisions.

- **Serving on a jury:** From time to time, you may be called to serve on a jury for the trial of other residents. Jury duty is an opportunity for citizens to participate in the legal process by helping decide the outcome of cases brought to trial. Therefore, it is important that you know the laws.

- **Abiding by laws:** Following laws is very important. As you will learn, Congress passes laws for the good of the nation.

- **Changing bad laws:** If you feel that laws are outdated or do not positively affect the United States, you must work to change the laws.

- **Supporting and defending the United States:** When other countries act aggressively or unjustly and the United States takes military action, citizens must support their nation. In some cases, this may entail enlisting in the military and fighting to defend the United States.

Disadvantages

There are a few potential disadvantages to applying for citizenship. They include:

- **Relinquishing citizenship to other nations:** In the "Oath of Allegiance," a naturalized citizen must renounce citizenship to all other nations. This also means that you can no longer fight for your country of origin during wartime; you must represent the United States militarily in times of conflict.

- **Facing potential dual citizenship problems:** Some nations recognize dual citizenship, which is citizenship in two countries. However, not all nations recognize dual citizenship.

Every resident of the United States should understand our country's government and history. The well-informed citizen is usually happier, better adjusted, more prosperous, and much more valuable to his community, state, and nation.

From the USCIS Sample Questions

Question: What Immigration and Naturalization Service form is used to apply to become a naturalized citizen?
Answer: Form N-400, "Application to File Petition for Naturalization."

Question: Name one benefit of being a citizen of the United States.
Answer: Obtain federal government jobs; travel with a United States passport; petition for close relatives to come to the United States to live.

LESSON 1

The Fifty States

As you will learn in this book, the United States began as a group of English colonies. When these colonies declared and won their independence from England, they became the first 13 states in the Union, or the United States. As more states joined the Union, the United States became larger. There are now 50 states in the Union, which means that there are 50 states in the United States.

The central government headquarters for the United States is in Washington, D.C., or the District of Columbia, located adjacent to Maryland and Virginia. The United States Capitol, the place where Congress meets, is located in Washington, D.C. The White House, the President's official home, is also located in Washington, D.C. The White House is located at 1600 Pennsylvania Avenue NW, Washington, D.C.

The United States is a large country on the continent of North America. Canada touches its northern border, and Mexico touches its southern border. The United States reaches from the Pacific Ocean on the west to the Atlantic Ocean on the east. There are 48 states that are joined together in the continental United States, and there are two other states that do not geographically border the other 48 states. Alaska is a very northern state that borders Canada, and Hawaii is a group of islands in the Pacific Ocean. Although disconnected from the rest of the country, Alaska and Hawaii are still states. Alaska and Hawaii were the 49th and 50th states of the Union.

The United States is very diverse. It has many different climates, geological formations, agricultural products, and natural resources. The United States has a great variety and abundance of vegetable and mineral products, excellent transportation systems, and one of the best organized governments in existence. No state looks the same or has the same conditions, and each state is unique.

The people of the United States are also very diverse. They work in many different types of industries and businesses and live in different kinds of homes and communities. Many people have immigrated recently to the United States, while other people have ancestors who immigrated hundreds of years ago. Diversity is one of the finest attributes of the Union and its 50 states. Despite these distinctions, every person living in the United States is still entitled to the same rights and responsibilities.

Fun Facts about the United States

Number of states: 50

Order that states entered the Union: Delaware, Pennsylvania, New Jersey, Georgia, Connecticut, Massachusetts, Maryland, South Carolina, New Hampshire, Virginia, New York, North Carolina, Rhode Island, Vermont, Kentucky, Tennessee, Ohio, Louisiana, Indiana, Mississippi, Illinois, Alabama, Maine, Missouri, Arkansas, Michigan, Florida, Texas, Iowa, Wisconsin, California, Minnesota, Oregon, Kansas, West Virginia, Nevada, Nebraska, Colorado, North Dakota, South Dakota, Montana, Washington, Idaho, Wyoming, Utah, Oklahoma, New Mexico, Arizona, Alaska, and Hawaii.

National capital: Washington, D.C.

Maximum elevation: Mt. McKinley, Alaska
—20,320 feet above sea level

Minimum elevation: Death Valley, California
—230 feet below sea level

Longest river in the United States: Mississippi River

Names of the Great Lakes: Huron, Ontario, Michigan, Erie, and Superior

Natural wonders and attractions: Grand Canyon, Niagara Falls, Mammoth Cave, the Painted Desert, Glacier National Park, Yellowstone National Park, Yosemite Valley, Death Valley, Mt. Rainier

From the USCIS Sample Questions

Question: How many states are there in the Union?
Answer: 50.

Question: How many states are there in the United States?
Answer: 50.

Question: What are the 49th and 50th states of the Union?
Answer: Alaska and Hawaii.

Question: What is the United States Capitol?
Answer: The place where Congress meets.

Question: Where does Congress meet?
Answer: In the Capitol in Washington, D.C.

Question: What is the White House?
Answer: The President's official home.

Question: What is the name of the President's official home?
Answer: The White House.

Question: Where is the White House located?
Answer: 1600 Pennsylvania Avenue NW, Washington, D.C.

For Further Study

Question: What is the largest river in the United States?
Answer: The Mississippi River.

Question: What are the Great Lakes?
Answer: Lakes Huron, Ontario, Michigan, Erie, and Superior.

Question: Name one of the natural wonders in the United States.
Answer: The Grand Canyon; Niagara Falls; Mammoth Cave; the Painted Desert; Glacier National Park; Yellowstone National Park; Yosemite Valley; Death Valley; Mt. Rainier.

American Symbols and Holidays

The American Flag

In 1777, a patriotic woman named Betsy Ross created the first American flag. The first flag had each of the original 13 states, represented by both a stripe and a star.

Our flag, sometimes called Old Glory, still has stars and stripes, but it has changed over time. The flag still has 13 stripes; each stripe represents the original 13 states. The stripes alternate red and white. The flag now has 50 stars; each star represents one state in the Union. The stars are white on a blue background.

Our flag floats over every public building and inside every schoolroom. The flag should be raised at sunrise and lowered at sunset. The American flag should always have the place of honor when carried with other flags. There is a national holiday, Flag Day, that celebrates the flag and the American ideals that it represents.

Songs and Writings

There are several important songs and writings that are sung and repeated in conjunction with flag recognition. The national anthem of the United States is called the Star-Spangled Banner. It was written on September 14, 1814 by Francis Scott Key; he was inspired by a flag he saw waving over Fort McHenry in the War of 1812. The lyrics to the Star-Spangled Banner can be found in Appendix D.

Citizens state the Pledge of Allegiance with their right hands over their heart to show their honor. The words to the Pledge of Allegiance are as follows: "I pledge allegiance to the flag of the United States of America, and to the republic for which it stands; one nation under God, indivisible, with liberty and justice for all."

Holidays

New Year's Day
January 1
Celebrates the arrival of the new calendar year

Martin Luther King, Jr. Day
3rd Monday of January
Commemorates a renowned civil rights leader, Martin Luther King, Jr., who used nonviolence to attain civil liberties for all Americans

Presidents' Day
3rd Monday in February
Recognizes the efforts of all past Presidents

Easter
Occurs on a Sunday in springtime, varies by year
Celebrates the resurrection of Jesus Christ *(religious holiday)*

Memorial Day
4th Monday of May
Honors all Americans who have died, especially those who have died in American wars

Flag Day
June 14
Recognizes the flag as an American symbol

Independence Day
July 4
Observes the Declaration of Independence on July 4th, 1776 and the beginning of the United States as a free and separate nation from England

Labor Day
1st Monday of September
Honors hard-working Americans

Columbus Day
Occurs on the 2nd Monday in October
Remembers the voyages of Christopher Columbus and his discovery of the New World, part of which later became the United States

Veterans Day	*November 11* Celebrates all veterans from American wars and conflicts
Thanksgiving	*4th Thursday in November* Commemorates the first Thanksgiving of the Pilgrims and Native Americans in 1621
Christmas	*December 25* Observes the birth of Jesus Christ *(religious holiday)*

From the USCIS Sample Questions

Question: What are the colors of our flag?
Answer: Red, white, and blue.

Question: How many stripes are there in the flag?
Answer: 13.

Question: What color are the stripes?
Answer: Red and white.

Question: What do the stripes on the flag mean?
Answer: They represent the original 13 states.

Question: How many stars are there in our flag?
Answer: 50.

Question: What color are the stars on our flag?
Answer: White.

Question: What do the stars on the flag mean?
Answer: One for each state in the Union.

Question: What is the national anthem of the United States?
Answer: The Star-Spangled Banner.

Question: Who wrote the Star-Spangled Banner?
Answer: Francis Scott Key.

Question: Who was Martin Luther King, Jr.?
Answer: A civil rights leader.

For Further Study

Question: Who created the first American flag?
Answer: Betsy Ross.

Question: What did the original American flag look like?
Answer: To represent the original 13 states, it had 13 red and white stripes and 13 white stars on a blue background.

Question: State the Pledge of Allegiance.
Answer: "I pledge allegiance to the flag of the United States of America, and to the republic for which it stands; one nation under God, indivisible, with liberty and justice for all."

Early American History

Summary of Dates

1000	Vikings discovered America
1492	Columbus discovered America
1565	Spanish founded St. Augustine, Florida
1607	English founded Jamestown, Virginia
1609	Dutch founded New Amsterdam, now known as New York
1619	Slavery introduced into Virginia
1620	English Pilgrims founded Plymouth, Massachusetts
1620–1720	People from many nations emigrated from Europe to America
1763	Last American war between English and French ended in British victory
	England established 13 colonies

Early Settlement and Colonization

The United States is a relatively new nation. Several hundred years ago, the United States did not exist, and the region was much less populated than it is now. The people who occupied the land hundreds of years ago originally crossed the Bering Strait that once connected Asia and North America. Called Indians by the first Europeans who arrived here, these people sustained themselves by hunting, fishing, and harvesting native plants. Many of these native groups had advanced agricultural systems, hunting and fishing methods, and cultural and spiritual practices. However, there was no centralized government that connected the Indians—now called American Indians or Native Americans—on a large geographical scale.

The history of the United States begins with the immigration of Europeans to North America. It is unknown when they officially arrived on this continent. Evidence suggests that Vikings, from the

Scandinavian region of northern Europe, landed on the North Atlantic coast around the year 1000, but did not establish permanent settlement. We usually attribute the discovery of North America to Christopher Columbus and his 1492 voyage to find a shorter and faster trade route to India and Asia, which had spices, raw materials, and ideas that Europeans desired. Sailing three ships, the *Nina,* the *Pinta,* and the *Santa Maria,* he landed on the North American continent and claimed the land in the name of Spain. Among the noted explorers to the New World was an Italian named Amerigo Vespucci, who made several maps and wrote letters describing his explorations. The New World was called America as a tribute to Vespucci.

Following Columbus' voyage, many countries sent expeditions to sail to North America. Spain, England, Holland, France, and Sweden sent people to explore, colonize, and settle in North America. **Spain** made the first permanent settlement at St. Augustine, Florida, in 1565. The first permanent **English** settlement was at Jamestown, Virginia, in 1607. The farmers in Virginia found it difficult to find enough laborers for their plantations, and began buying African slaves from traders in 1619. In 1609, the **Dutch** made a settlement at New Amsterdam, which is now New York. **French** fur traders and missionaries explored Canada, the Mississippi River Valley, and the Great Lakes region. **Sweden** sent explorers and colonists to the Delaware area, and many Swedes established permanent residence in what became Minnesota and Wisconsin.

The Pilgrims

In 1620, a band of English people who are now called the Pilgrims traveled to America for religious freedom. A ship called the *Mayflower* brought the Pilgrims to America. They established a settlement at Plymouth, Massachusetts. The Pilgrims had a difficult time adjusting to life in the New World, and many died from illness, hunger, and cold. Fortunately, the American Indians (Native Americans), who had successful hunting and agricultural skills, helped the Pilgrims in America. To recognize their friendship, the American Indians and the Pilgrims had a feast of thanksgiving. The Thanksgiving feast was celebrated for the first time by the American colonists, and we now celebrate Thanksgiving every year in memory of this historic relationship.

War in Europe and America

While Europeans established colonies in America, England and France were constantly at war. Ultimately, this war spread to the New World. The English and French colonies engaged in four separate wars. In 1763, England won a complete victory and was left in control of most of the land east of the Mississippi, including the colonies on the Atlantic coast. They also won Canada, which is still part of the British Commonwealth. England established 13 colonies, which they called New England. These colonies eventually became the original 13 states of the United States: Connecticut, New Hampshire, New York, New Jersey, Massachusetts, Pennsylvania, Delaware, Virginia, North Carolina, South Carolina, Georgia, Rhode Island, and Maryland.

From the USCIS Sample Questions

Question: Why did the Pilgrims come to America?
Answer: For religious freedom.

Question: What is the name of the ship that brought the Pilgrims to America?
Answer: The *Mayflower*.

Question: Who helped the Pilgrims in America?
Answer: The American Indians (Native Americans).

Question: What holiday was celebrated for the first time by the American colonists?
Answer: Thanksgiving.

Question: What were the 13 original states of the United States called?
Answer: Colonies.

Question: Can you name the 13 original states?
Answer: Connecticut, New Hampshire, New York, New Jersey, Massachusetts, Pennsylvania, Delaware, Virginia, North Carolina, South Carolina, Georgia, Rhode Island, and Maryland.

For Further Study

Question: When did the first Europeans travel to North America?
Answer: Approximately the year 1000.

Question: To whom do we attribute the discovery of America?
Answer: Christopher Columbus.

Question: How did America receive its name?
Answer: From Amerigo Vespucci, a noted explorer who made maps and wrote articles describing the New World.

Question: What main nations made settlements in America?
Answer: Spain, England, France, Holland, and Sweden.

Question: What was the final result of the wars between England and France in America?
Answer: The English won a complete victory and established 13 American colonies.

LESSON 4

Revolutionary War

Summary of Dates

1775	Continental Congress formed
July 4th, 1776	Declaration of Independence issued, start of Revolutionary War
1781	Last battle of the Revolutionary War
1783	Peace treaty signed between United States and England
	United States became a free nation

The Revolutionary War, 1776–1783

Countries engaged:	13 colonies (afterward known as United States) against Great Britain; the colonies were assisted by France
Cause:	"No taxation without representation"
Result:	The United States secured its independence
Leaders	
American:	George Washington, Patrick Henry, Thomas Jefferson, Benjamin Franklin
English:	Lord Cornwallis

Frustration in the Colonies

By the late 1700s, England had 13 well-established colonies in America. Although the colonists sought opportunity, they were restrained by English rule. On the continent of North America, they expected to pray and work freely, without English influence or restraint. However, English laws regulated the affairs of the colonies. England heavily taxed the colonists, prohibited trade with other countries, and permitted trade only with English ships. Colonies could not send representatives to English Parliament to help make the laws. Many colonists felt that they should not pay taxes unless they could be fairly represented. "No taxation without representation" became the slogan for their frustration. To compel the colonists to pay taxes and obey laws, the English government sent soldiers to the colonies, and required colonists to feed and house the soldiers. Instead of bringing peace, there was constant unrest between the soldiers and the colonists.

The Continental Congress and the Declaration of Independence

Some of the leading colonists decided to take a stand against England. In 1775, the **Continental Congress**, a group of delegates from the colonies, convened and decided to fight until England gave them more representation. Ultimately, they decided that representation was insufficient; they wanted a new nation, free from English rule. On July 4, 1776, the Continental Congress adopted the **Declaration of Independence**, stating the basic belief that all men are created equal. Thomas Jefferson, one of America's famous statesmen, was the main writer of the Declaration of Independence. The text of the Declaration of Independence can be found in Appendix F. Another statesman, Patrick Henry, is famous for his revolutionary cry, "Give me liberty, or give me death!"

The Revolutionary War

After the colonists declared independence, the war between the two countries became known as the Revolutionary War. The colonies fought England during the Revolutionary War to establish their own nation. The Continental Congress selected George Washington to be the first Commander-in-Chief of the United States military. Washington eventually became our first President. In terms of external support, France significantly helped the colonists battle England by providing valuable aid to the Americans.

The last engagement of the war was in 1781, when the British commander, Lord Cornwallis, surrendered at Yorktown, Virginia. Shortly afterward, all British armies withdrew from the United States. The two governments signed a peace treaty in 1783, and the United States became a free nation later that year.

Every year, American citizens celebrate Independence Day on the 4th of July, in memory of the adoption of the Declaration of Independence on July 4th, 1776. Independence Day celebrates American independence from England, and the establishment of the United States of America as a free and independent nation.

Question: When was the Declaration of Independence adopted?
Answer: July 4, 1776.

Question: What is the basic belief of the Declaration of Independence?
Answer: That all men are created equal.

Question: Who was the main writer of the Declaration of Independence?
Answer: Thomas Jefferson.

Question: Which President was the first Commander-in-Chief of the United States military?
Answer: George Washington.

Question: What country did we fight during the Revolutionary War?
Answer: England.

Question: Who said, "Give me liberty, or give me death!"?
Answer: Patrick Henry.

Question: What is the 4th of July?
Answer: Independence Day.

Question: What is the date of Independence Day?
Answer: July 4.

Question: Independence Day celebrates American independence from whom?
Answer: England.

For Further Study

Question: Why did the colonies become dissatisfied with English rule?
Answer: Taxation without representation in English Parliament; the inability to create commerce independent from England; quartering of English soldiers.

Question: What was the initial motivation for the colonies' fighting?
Answer: Initially, representative government. Later, complete independence.

Question: What country aided the United States in the Revolutionary War?
Answer: France.

Question: When did the Revolutionary War end?
Answer: The English surrendered in 1781. The peace treaty was signed in 1783.

LESSON 5

Making of the Constitution

The Articles of Confederation

After the Declaration of Independence on July 4th, 1776, a Congress, composed of delegates from the 13 colonies, formulated a plan of government for their new nation. They wanted to have a **republic**, a government by the people through their elected representatives. The Congress called their system of laws the Articles of Confederation.

The citizens of the new nation soon discovered that the Articles of Confederation were not satisfactory. One problem was that there was no President or executive head. Also, Congress could make laws but could not enforce them. Moreover, any state could easily withdraw from the Union if it wished to do so.

After a few years, the people decided to improve the Articles of Confederation. Although they first hoped to revise the Articles of Confederation, they soon decided that they should create an entirely new Constitution. The Constitution was written in 1787. Many of the most capable men in the new nation were members of the convention that wrote the Constitution. George Washington, Alexander Hamilton, James Madison, and Benjamin Franklin are some of the notable representatives who were present.

The Constitution

The delegates who drafted the Constitution had several points of disagreement. One of the key issues to be resolved was representation of states' interests. Some states were large and some were small; some were agricultural and some commercial; some were slave states and some free. The Constitution created a compromise for these differences by establishing a **bicameral** legislature, or two houses in Congress. In the Senate, all states have equal representation; in the House of Representatives, the representation depends upon population. In both houses, every member has an independent vote.

Slavery was another important issue in the creation of the Constitution. The southern states had a substantial number of slaves, while the northern states did not; this affected issues of taxation for and representation of slaves. Ultimately, the Three-Fifths compromise enabled each slave to be counted as three-fifths of a person to determine representation. This compromise also forbade slave importation after 1808. Although the states had differences, the Constitution created a nation in which all states were able to compromise and benefit.

The Constitution is the supreme law of the land. The introduction to the Constitution is called the Preamble. Most Americans are quite familiar with the first sentence of the Preamble: "We the People of the United States. . . ." The Constitution emphasizes the principles of liberty, equality, and justice that we cherish. Everyone—both citizens and non-citizens living in the United States—have rights that are guaranteed by the Constitution and the Bill of Rights. The new Constitution was a great improvement over the Articles of Confederation. Indeed, it is so excellent that, although over 200 years have passed since its adoption, there have been only 27 amendments to the original Constitution.

From the USCIS Sample Questions

Question: What is the introduction to the Constitution called?
Answer: The Preamble.

Question: What is the Constitution?
Answer: The supreme law of the land.

Question: What is the supreme law of the United States?
Answer: The Constitution.

Question: In what year was the Constitution written?
Answer: 1787.

Question: Whose rights are guaranteed by the Constitution and the Bill of Rights?
Answer: Everyone (citizens and non-citizens living in the United States).

For Further Study

Question: Upon what principles is the United States Constitution based?
Answer: Liberty, equality, and justice.

Question: What was the first system of laws of the United States called?
Answer: The Articles of Confederation.

Question: Why were the Articles of Confederation unsatisfactory?
Answer: For several reasons: there was no President; Congress could make laws but could not enforce them; any state could withdraw from the Union if it chose.

LESSON 6
Constitutional Amendments

The Constitution is the supreme law of the United States. However, the Constitution can be changed. We call a change to the Constitution an **amendment**. There are 27 changes, or amendments, to the Constitution.

There are two ways to pass an amendment to the Constitution. In the first method, an amendment must pass both houses of Congress by a two-thirds majority vote, then must be **ratified**, or approved, by three-fourths of the state legislatures. In the other method, the states may request a convention called by Congress at the request of the states; however, this method has never been used.

Twenty-seven amendments have been passed by Congress and ratified by the states. The first ten amendments to the Constitution, known as the **Bill of Rights**, were passed in 1791. They ensure many important individual freedoms to citizens and non-citizens of the United States. The first amendment guarantees the freedoms of speech, press, religion, peaceable assembly, and petition to change government. The freedom of speech—one of the most fundamental rights in this country—comes from the Bill of Rights.

The following is a summary of the Bill of Rights:

1. The right to freedom of speech, press, religion, peaceable assembly, and petition to change government.

2. The right to bear arms (the right to have weapons or own a gun).

3. The government may not quarter, or house, soldiers in the people's homes during peacetime without the people's consent.

4. "Unlawful search and seizure": The government may not search or take a person's property without a warrant.

5. "Double jeopardy": A person may not be tried twice for the same crime and also does not have to testify against himself.

During a trial, a person may "plead the fifth," which means that he is using the fifth amendment to protect himself from self-incrimination.

6. "Free and fair trial": A person charged with a crime still has some rights, such as the right to a trial and to have a lawyer.

7. A person has a right to trial by jury in most cases.

8. People have protection against excessive or unreasonable fines, as well as from cruel and unusual punishment.

9. The people have rights other than those mentioned in the Constitution.

10. Any power not given to the federal government by the Constitution is a power of either the state or the people.

From the USCIS Sample Questions

Question: Can the Constitution be changed?
Answer: Yes.

Question: What do we call a change to the Constitution?
Answer: An amendment.

Question: How many changes or amendments are there to the Constitution?
Answer: 27.

Question: What are the first 10 amendments to the Constitution called?
Answer: The Bill of Rights.

Question: What is the Bill of Rights?
Answer: The first 10 amendments of the Constitution.

Question: Where does the freedom of speech come from?
Answer: The Bill of Rights.

Question: Name one right guaranteed by the first amendment.
Answer: Freedom of: speech, press, religion, peaceable assembly, and petition to change government.

Question: Name three rights or freedoms guaranteed by the Bill of Rights.

Answer: Any three of the following freedoms: 1. The right of freedom of speech, press, religion, peaceable assembly, and petition to change government. 2. The right to bear arms (the right to have weapons or own a gun, though subject to certain regulations). 3. The government may not quarter, or house, soldiers in the people's homes during peacetime without the people's consent. 4. The government may not search or take a person's property without a warrant. 5. A person may not be tried twice for the same crime and does not have to testify against himself. 6. A person charged with a crime still has some rights, such as the right to a trial and to have a lawyer. 7. A person has a right to trial by jury in most cases. 8. The protection against excessive or unreasonable fines or cruel and unusual punishment. 9. The people have rights other than those mentioned in the Constitution. 10. Any power not given to the federal government by the Constitution is a power of either the state or the people.

For Further Study

Question: How is an amendment usually made?
Answer: An amendment must pass both houses of Congress by a two-thirds majority vote, and must then be ratified by the legislatures of three-fourths of the states.

Question: Does the President sign amendments?
Answer: No.

Nineteenth Century History

Summary of Dates

1812–1814	War of 1812
1846–1848	Mexican War
1861–1865	Civil War
1898	Spanish-American War

Americans can be proud that many of the wars in which the United States has fought have been on behalf of freedom. Thousands of American soldiers who have given their lives in these battles have not died in vain. Every declared conflict has resulted in a victory for the United States and our allies. Not only have Americans secured and maintained their independence, but the people of many other countries have gained freedom through American help. In the Nineteenth century, the United States engaged in the following wars:

The War of 1812, 1812–1814

Countries engaged: United States and Great Britain
Cause: Dispute over "the freedom of the seas"
Result: United States won commercial independence
Leaders
  American: Commodore Perry, General Andrew Jackson

The Mexican War, 1846–1848

Countries engaged: United States and Mexico
Cause: Dispute over the boundary line between the two countries
Result: Settlement of boundary line between the United States and Mexico, addition of New Mexico and California to United States territory

Leaders
   American: General Zachary Taylor, Major Fremont,
                          General Kearney, General Scott

The Civil War, 1861–1865

Country engaged: The northern and southern United States (the
                      "North" or "Union" versus the "South" or
                      "Confederacy")
Cause: Slavery, states' rights, secession of the southern
                      states from the Union
Results: The abolition of slavery and preservation of the
                      Union. Abraham Lincoln was President during
                      the Civil War. He issued the **Emancipation
                      Proclamation**, an announcement that freed
                      many slaves.
Leaders
   Union: President Abraham Lincoln, General Grant,
                        General Sherman, General Sheridan, General
                        McClellan, General Mead
   Confederacy: President Jefferson Davis, General Lee, General
                        Jackson, General Johnston

The Spanish-American War, 1898

Countries engaged: United States and Spain
Cause: Spanish tyranny in Cuba, the blowing up of the
                      United States battleship *Maine*
Results: Puerto Rico, Guam, and the Philippines were
                      ceded to United States by Spain, Cuba became
                      independent
Leaders
   American: President William McKinley, Admiral Dewey,
                        Colonel Roosevelt, Admiral Sampson,
                        Commodore Schley, General Wood, General
                        Miles

From the USCIS Sample Questions

Question: Which President freed the slaves?
Answer: Abraham Lincoln.

Question: Who was the President during the Civil War?
Answer: Abraham Lincoln.

Question: What did the Emancipation Proclamation do?
Answer: Freed many slaves.

For Further Review

Question: What was the result of the War of 1812?
Answer: Commercial independence for the United States.

Question: What was the cause of the Mexican War of 1846–1848?
Answer: Dispute over the boundary between Mexico and the United States.

Question: Name one reason for the Civil War.
Answer: Slavery, states' rights, the secession of the southern states from the Union.

Twentieth and Twenty-First Century History

Summary of Dates

1917–1918	World War I
1941–1945	World War II
1950–1953	Korean Conflict
1961–1975	Vietnam Conflict
1991	Persian Gulf War
2003	War in Iraq

In the Twentieth and Twenty-First Centuries, the United States engaged in the following wars and conflicts:

Declared Wars

World War I, 1917–1918

Countries engaged:	United States, Great Britain, France, and their allies against Germany and its allies
Cause:	Germany's ambition for power and expansion of territory
Result:	The curbing of Germany's ambition, overthrow of German government, liberation of several small nations
Leaders	
Allies:	President Woodrow Wilson, General Pershing, Marshal Foch, Marshal Haig
German-Austrian:	Kaiser Wilhelm, Emperor Charles, General von Ludendorff, Marshal von Hindenburg

World War II, 1941–1945

Countries engaged: *The Allies*—Twenty-six allied nations including United States, Great Britain, Russia, and their allies

The Axis Powers—Three allied nations of Germany, Italy, and Japan

Cause: Germany and Japanese aggression and expansion, Italian fascism and German Nazism, the Holocaust

Result: Allied victory, dissolution of the German empire, destruction of Hiroshima and Nagasaki from nuclear attacks, end of the Holocaust and internment of Jews, and establishment of the United Nations*

Leaders

Allies: President Franklin D. Roosevelt, General Dwight D. Eisenhower, General Charles De Gaulle, Prime Minister Winston Churchill, Joseph Stalin

Axis: Adolf Hitler, Benito Mussolini

Persian Gulf War, 1991

Countries engaged: Coalition of thirty-two nations including United States, Britain, Egypt, France, and Saudi Arabia; Iraq

Cause: Iraq's invasion of Kuwait and refusal to withdraw peaceably

*Note: As an outcome of World War II, representatives from many countries worldwide established the **United Nations** to promote international peace, cooperation, security, and human rights in 1945. The purposes of the United Nations are for countries to discuss and try to resolve world problems, and to provide economic aid to many countries. The United Nations now contains 191 countries that work together to help mediate issues of international importance. It is not a legislative body; rather, it is a group of nations that strive to create viable and sound solutions to matters of international significance.

Result:	Massive bombings of Iraq by coalition forces and ground attacks forced Iraq to surrender, United Nations Security Council placed sanctions against Iraq and laid out strict guidelines in order to remove the sanctions

Leaders

United States:	President George H. W. Bush, General Norman Schwarzkopf
Iraq:	President Saddam Hussein

War in Iraq, 2003

Countries engaged:	United States, Britain, and allies; Iraq
Cause:	Iraq's refusal to comply with sanctions (United Nations weapons inspections) outlined in the 1991 cease-fire agreement
Result:	United States attacked Iraq by air and ground, overthrew the Iraqi government, and removed Saddam Hussein

Leaders

United States:	President George W. Bush, Donald Rumsfeld
Britain:	Tony Blair
Iraq:	President Saddam Hussein

Undeclared Wars

Korean Conflict, 1950–1953

Countries engaged:	United Nations led by the United States; North Korean and Chinese Communists
Cause:	Invasion of South Korea by Communists in North Korea seen as an act of aggression and violation of the United Nations charter
Result:	Armistice, or peace agreement, signed in 1953, establishment of a neutral nations' supervisory commission

Leaders

American:	General Douglas MacArthur

Vietnam Conflict, 1961–1975

Countries engaged: United States, South Vietnam, North Vietnam, National Liberation Front, Vietcong guerrillas

Cause: Attempt to establish Communist rule in South Vietnam

Result: Cease-fire and removal of American troops from Vietnam in 1973, last American deaths in 1975, North Vietnamese establishment of Communism in South Vietnam

Leaders
   American: President John F. Kennedy, President Lyndon B. Johnson, President Richard M. Nixon, Henry Kissinger

From the USCIS Sample Questions

Question: Which countries were our enemies during World War II?
Answer: Germany, Italy, and Japan.

Question: Name one purpose of the United Nations.
Answer: For countries to discuss and try to resolve world problems; to provide economic aid to many countries.

For Further Study

Question: The United Nations was an outcome of which war?
Answer: WWII.

Question: Who was President during the Persian Gulf War of 1991?
Answer: George H. W. Bush.

Question: What does armistice mean?
Answer: Peace agreement.

LESSON 9

Federalism

Because the founders of this country were wary of tyrannical leaders, they established federalism, separation of powers, and checks and balances in an effort to prevent an abuse of power. **Federalism** decentralizes power by setting up different levels of authority. **Separation of powers** splits the functions of government into different branches. Similarly, a system of **checks and balances** allows these branches to verify the decisions of the other branches.

The United States government is the structure that provides order to this great nation. The Constitution of the United States established rules and regulations for the government to follow. The Constitution gives the government power to govern effectively and create positive changes. At the same time, it restrains the leaders so that they do not have too much power over the people.

We have a republican form of government. It is a **republic**, which means that the ultimate power lies in a body of citizens who elect accountable officers and representatives to manage the government.

Branches of Government

There are three branches in our government. They are the executive, legislative, and judicial branches. **Executive** means law-enforcing. In the United States, the executive branch of our federal government includes the President, the Cabinet, and the departments under the Cabinet members. **Legislative** means law-making. Congress is the legislative branch of the federal government. **Judicial** means law-interpreting or law-explaining. The Supreme Court and all federal courts are the judicial branch of our national government.

Levels of Government

In addition to the three branches of our government, there are several levels of government. First, there is the **federal**, or national, level, which is described above. There is also a **state** government level and a local government level, which includes both **county** and **city** government. These levels of government also have leaders who perform executive, legislative, and judicial duties on a smaller level.

Federal government provides military protection, personal freedom, citizenship rights, and postal service subsidies. These are uniform for people in all states. State government provides state institutions, educational privileges, highways, water rights, insurance regulations, railroad regulations, and game and wildlife protection. These are state issues because state governments can more accurately determine local needs. County government provides institutions for health and welfare, courts, jails, tax regulations, and public records. City government provides police and fire protection, street improvements, parks, playgrounds, and educational facilities. Decentralization ensures that individual citizens feel represented in this large and diverse nation.

From the USCIS Sample Questions

Question: What kind of government does the United States have?
Answer: Republican.

Question: How many branches are there in our government?
Answer: 3.

Question: What are the three branches of our government?
Answer: Executive, legislative, and judicial.

Question: What is the executive branch of our government?
Answer: The President, Cabinet, and departments under the Cabinet members.

Question: What is the legislative branch of our government?
Answer: Congress.

Question: What is the judicial branch of our government?
Answer: The Supreme Court and federal courts.

For Further Study

Question: What does executive mean?
Answer: Law-enforcing.

Question: What does legislative mean?
Answer: Law-making.

Question: What does judicial mean?
Answer: Law-explaining or law-interpreting.

Question: Name one thing that the national government provides.
Answer: National government provides naturalization laws, passports, military protection, personal freedom, and subsidizes the postal service.

Question: Name one thing that the state government provides.
Answer: State government provides many state institutions, educational privileges, state highways, insurance and railroad regulations, and protects game and wildlife.

Question: Name one thing that the local county government provides.
Answer: County government provides institutions for health and welfare, courts and jails, tax regulations, and public records.

Question: Name one thing that the local city government provides.
Answer: City government provides police and fire protection, street improvements, parks, playgrounds, and educational facilities.

Voting

The Right to Vote

A republic is a democracy in which the people elect representatives as well as a President as Chief Executive. In order to choose the leaders of the country, it is necessary for the citizens to vote at free and fair elections held on a regular basis. The right to vote is the most important right granted to United States citizens. The right to vote is also known as **suffrage**. Citizens should consider it a duty to vote for the officers and measures that they think are best for the country. Every qualified resident of this country should exercise the right to vote.

The minimum legal voting age in the United States is 18 years. In the United States, people must register before they can vote. In order to vote at a **primary election**, an election in which political parties nominate their candidates to run in the final presidential election held in November, the person who registers must declare which political party he belongs to, if any. The two major political parties in the United States are the Democratic and Republican parties. In general, the Democrats are more liberal, while the Republicans are more conservative. Although the two largest parties are Democratic and Republican, citizens may also register with a smaller party, or they may choose to be **nonpartisan**, which means that they are not affiliated with any particular political party. Here is a list of all the current political parties in the United States:

- Republican Party
- Democratic Party
- American Party
- Constitution Party
- Green Party
- Libertarian Party
- Natural Law Party

- Peace and Freedom Party
- Prohibition Party
- Reform Party
- Socialist Party USA
- Socialist Workers Party
- Independent (nonpartisan)

Voting and Elections

The election process extends throughout the year. People wishing to run for office must first file a declaration of candidacy. After filing this declaration, the candidate must then secure sponsors for his nomination. The number of sponsors required depends upon the nature of the office. A state may hold a caucus, which is where local political party members meet to discuss their preferences for the candidates running for public office. It may also hold a primary election, an election for the purpose of nominating candidates for office.

Primary elections for the presidency are held every four years. At these elections, political parties nominate their candidates for the presidential election in November. At the primary election, the candidate of each political party receiving the highest vote for each office becomes the political party's candidate at the general election. For nonpartisan offices, the two candidates who receive the highest votes at the primary election become candidates for each such office at the general election.

It is our duty to elect representatives who will serve our nation's needs. Many nations do not give citizens the option to vote in free and fair elections. Because we have the freedom to vote in this democratic process, it is important that citizens are knowledgeable about their candidates for office on federal, state, county, and local levels. Being educated about politics and the political leaders is one of the responsibilities of being a citizen in the United States.

Question: What is the most important right granted to United States citizens?
Answer: The right to vote.

Question: What are the two major political parties in the United States today?
Answer: Democratic and Republican.

Question: What is the minimum voting age in the United States?
Answer: Eighteen (18).

For Further Study

Question: Can any citizen who meets the minimum legal voting age vote in elections?
Answer: No, citizens must register before they can vote.

Question: What is a primary election?
Answer: A primary election is an election for the purpose of nominating party candidates for office.

LESSON 11

Election of the President

Requirements for Office

There are several important requirements to be eligible for presidency. The President must be a natural-born citizen. A President must be at least 35 years old when he is elected. Additionally, presidential candidates must also be residents of the United States for 14 years preceding the election.

The Electoral College

The people elect the President, but not directly. When the Constitution was written, the founders created the **Electoral College** to elect the President of the United States. It still exists today, although it has little independent authority, as the members are bound to cast their votes as per their party representation.

Political parties, such as the Republican, Democratic, and Green parties, form state organizations. The leaders of these parties choose the men and women of the Electoral College. In the Electoral College, the presidential electors pledge to vote for the candidate who is nominated for the presidency at their party's convention.

The number of electors in a state is equal to the number of House Representatives plus the number of Senators from that state. There are a total of 538 electors in the Electoral College, representing the 435 Representatives, 100 Senators, plus the 3 electors from the District of Columbia.

The President and Vice-President are voted for together on the same party ticket. The presidential electors pledge to vote for the candidate who is nominated for the presidency at their party's national convention. Therefore, it is known almost immediately after an election whether a candidate has a majority of votes in the Electoral College. If a candidate has a majority vote, he is elected. If no candidate has a majority, the members of the House of Representatives vote for President, with each state having only one vote. This rare process—election of the President via the House of Representatives—has only happened twice in American history.

Term of Office

We elect the President for four years. In the original Constitution, the President could serve as many terms as the people wished; since 1951 when the Twenty-Second Amendment was passed, a President may serve a maximum of two terms in office. Presidential elections are held every four years. Elections are held in November, and the President is **inaugurated**, or takes office, on the twentieth of January following his election. President George W. Bush, for example, was elected in 2000 and took office on January 20, 2001.

Presidential Succession

If the President dies, resigns, or is unable to continue his term, the Vice-President becomes President. If both President and Vice-President cannot serve as President, the Speaker of the House of Representatives succeeds to the office. Following the Speaker in the line of succession are: the President Pro Tempore of the Senate, the Secretary of State, the Secretary of Treasury, and other Cabinet members, as long as the successor is a native-born citizen.

From the USCIS Sample Questions

Question: According to the Constitution, a person must meet certain requirements in order to be eligible to become President. Name one of these requirements.
Answer: Must be a natural born citizen of the United States; must be at least 35 years old by the time he/she will serve; must have lived in the United States for at least 14 years.

Question: Who elects the President of the United States?
Answer: The Electoral College.

Question: For how long do we elect the President?
Answer: Four years.

Question: How many terms can a President serve?
Answer: Two.

Question: In what month do we vote for President?
Answer: November.

Question: In what month is the new President inaugurated?
Answer: January.

Question: Who becomes President of the United States if the President should die?
Answer: Vice-President.

For Further Study

Question: What is the total number of members in the Electoral College?
Answer: 538 presidential electors.

Question: Who elects a President if the Electoral College fails to do so?
Answer: If the Electoral College fails to elect a President, the House of Representatives must do so. Each state only has one vote.

Question: What is the present order of succession to the President?
Answer: President, Vice-President, Speaker of the House of Representatives, President Pro Tempore of the United States Senate, Secretary of State, Secretary of Treasury, then other Cabinet officers if qualified.

Question: When does the President take office?
Answer: The President takes office on the twentieth of January following his election.

LESSON 12

Presidential Powers

Powers of the President

As Chief Executive of the United States, the President is the most powerful and visible person in the entire nation. Moreover, because the United States is such an influential nation, the President may therefore be the most powerful figure in the world.

The President has many important powers and duties. The Constitution outlines his primary roles and responsibilities. The President:

- Is Chief Executive and sees that our nation's laws are enforced.

- Signs bills into law; also **vetoes**—objects to—bills sent from Congress.

- Is Commander-in-Chief of the United States military.

- Grants pardons for offenses against United States laws.

- Delivers an annual message to Congress and the people called the State of the Union, which outlines what he thinks are the nation's needs and concerns.

- Calls special sessions of Congress when necessary.

- Fills vacancies in certain offices.

- Appoints members of the Cabinet and judges of the United States courts.

- Makes international treaties and appoints ambassadors and consuls to foreign countries to ensure diplomatic relations with other nations.

In addition to the powers outlined in the Constitution, the President has many other responsibilities to his country. For instance, he must act as a liaison to the rest of the world and represent the United States citizens' interests on an international scale. Because it is a world power, the United States must play a primary role in facilitating peace, ensuring human rights, and promoting democracy abroad. The President must also provide wisdom and support to the United States in times of crisis. These roles are important to help the nation run smoothly.

Checks and Balances

The Constitution also provides checks and balances on the executive branch. For example, before a bill can become a law, a majority of both houses of Congress must approve the bill. The President may then sign the bill to adopt its legislation, or he may veto the bill if he disapproves. If the President vetoes the bill, then two-thirds of Congress must approve its passage; otherwise, the measure does not become a law. In addition, the judicial branch may try a case in the Supreme Court to judge whether or not the law is constitutional. This system ensures that all three branches of our national government consider the bills to be just and beneficial for the nation. Similarly, although the President is the Commander-in-Chief of the military, only Congress can declare war. Moreover, Congress must provide consent to all presidential appointments.

Notable Presidents

We have had 43 Presidents of the United States. The complete list of Presidents and their dates in office can be found in Appendix I. Below are descriptions of several notable American Presidents.

George Washington was the first President of the United States. He became President in 1789 and served two terms. Because of his role as Commander-in-Chief of the military in the Revolutionary War, and because he was our first President, he is also called the "father of our country."

From 1861 to 1865, Abraham Lincoln served as President. Lincoln was our 16th President. His presidency occurred during the Civil War, in which the southern states seceded from the Union. Lincoln is remembered for helping defeat the Confederacy during the Civil War, keeping the United States intact, and issuing the Gettysburg Address that freed the slaves in the southern states. Lincoln delivered his famous Gettysburg Address in November 1863 at the dedication of the Gettysburg battlefield as a national cemetery. In this address, Lincoln called a republic "a government of the people, by the people, and for the people." The text of the Gettysburg Address is in Appendix H.

George W. Bush is the President of the United States today. He has served one term in office. President Bush will run for a second presidential term in the next election in November 2004.

Question: Who is the Commander-in-Chief of the United States military?
Answer: The President.

Question: Who signs bills into law?
Answer: The President.

Question: Who was the first President of the United States?
Answer: George Washington.

Question: Which President is called the "father of our country"?
Answer: George Washington.

Question: Who is the President of the United States today?
Answer: George W. Bush.

For Further Study

Question: Who is the Chief Executive of the United States?
Answer: The President.

Question: How many Presidents have we had in the United States?
Answer: 43.

Question: Who was President during the Civil War?
Answer: Abraham Lincoln.

Question: Who called a republic "a government of the people, by the people, and for the people"?
Answer: Abraham Lincoln.

LESSON 13

The President's Cabinet

The Cabinet is a special group of the executive branch that advises the President. In the Cabinet, many of the departments have several divisions called Bureaus. The heads of the departments are the chief advisors to the President. In the following list, the Cabinet officers are arranged in alphabetical order by office.

The members of the Cabinet do not need to be born in the United States to serve; however, they must be natural-born citizens to succeed to the presidency. The President appoints members of the Cabinet, and the Senate confirms these appointments. These are the members of President George W. Bush's Cabinet:

- Attorney General, Department of Justice—John Ashcroft
- Secretary of Agriculture—Ann M. Veneman
- Secretary of Commerce—Don Evans
- Secretary of Defense—Donald Rumsfeld
- Secretary of Education—Rod Paige
- Secretary of Energy—Spencer Abraham
- Secretary of Health and Human Services—Tommy Thompson
- Office of Homeland Security Adviser—Tom Ridge
- Secretary of Housing and Urban Development—Mel Martinez
- Secretary of the Interior—Gale Norton
- Secretary of Labor—Elaine Chao
- Secretary of State—Colin Powell
- Secretary of Transportation—Norman Mineta
- Secretary of Treasury—John Snow
- Secretary of Veterans Affairs—Anthony Principi
- Vice-President—Dick Cheney

Additionally, President George W. Bush has also given Cabinet-status appointments to the Administrator of the Environmental Protection Agency, the Director of the Office of Management and Budget, the Director of National Drug Control Policy, and the United States Trade Representative.

Duties of the Cabinet Advisers

The **Secretary of Agriculture** controls the improvement of agricultural conditions. The Bureau of Soils, the Bureau of Markets, the Forest Service, the Dairy Industry, and Plant Quarantine are among the important divisions of this department.

The **Secretary of Commerce** supervises trade relations both domestically and internationally. Some of the divisions are the Bureau of Foreign and Domestic Commerce, Census Bureau, Patent Office, Bureau of Public Roads, and the Weather Bureau.

The **Secretary of Defense** is the head of a department that consolidates the affairs of the Army, the Air Force, the Navy, and the Marines.

The **Secretary of Education** supervises all the committees concerned with education.

The **Secretary of Energy** supervises and coordinates the following agencies: the Federal Energy Board, the Energy Research and Development Administration, and the Federal Power Commission.

The **Secretary of Health and Human Services** is in charge of the Social Security Administration, Public Health Service, Children's Bureau, and Women's Bureau.

The **Office of Homeland Security** was created by President George W. Bush after the terrorist attacks on the United States on September 11th, 2001. This department protects our national borders, regulates travel into and out of the country, and is charged with preventing future terrorist attacks. It also oversees the United States Citizenship and Immigration Services (USCIS), which controls immigration and naturalization.

The **Secretary of Housing and Urban Development** supervises and coordinates various organizations dealing with housing construction and financing. This department also oversees housing rights issues on a federal level.

The **Secretary of the Interior** manages many important affairs within the United States. Among the departments are the Bureau of

Mines, the Office of Indian Affairs, the National Park Service, and the Fish and Wildlife Service.

The **Secretary of Labor** directs important affairs concerning labor. The Bureau of Labor Statistics and Veterans' Reemployment Rights are part of this department.

The **Secretary of State** is in charge of our diplomatic relations with foreign countries. This department oversees the control of passports and the relations with consuls and ambassadors. The Secretary of State is also the head of the Cabinet.

The **Secretary of Transportation** supervises and coordinates activities of the National Transportation Safety Board, U.S. Coast Guard, Federal Aviation Administration, Federal Highway Administration, Federal Railroad Administration, and the St. Lawrence Seaway Development Corporation.

The **Secretary of the Treasury** controls the financial affairs of the United States. Included in this department are: the Bureau of Engraving and Printing, the control of Mints, the United States Secret Service, and Internal Revenue Service.

The **Secretary of Veterans Affairs** oversees national matters concerning United States veterans and their dependents. These benefits include health provisions, financial aid, educational support, housing help, and burial assistance for veterans and their families.

The **Attorney General**, whose department is often called the **Department of Justice**, is the United States lawyer. The Attorney General is the legal adviser of the other Cabinet members. He is in charge of United States prisons.

From the USCIS Sample Questions

Question: What special group advises the President?
Answer: The Cabinet.

Question: Who is the Vice-President of the United States today?
Answer: Dick Cheney.

For Further Study

Question: What is the Cabinet?
Answer: A body of people who assist the President in his executive duties.

Question: How do Cabinet officers obtain their positions?
Answer: Appointed by the President, with the consent of the Senate.

Question: Which Cabinet office oversees the United States Citizenship and Immigration Services?
Answer: The Office of Homeland Security.

Congressional Powers and Law-Making

Powers of Congress

Congress is composed of the Senate and the House of Representatives. The people elect Congress to make this nation's laws. The power of law-making is expressly given to Congress in the Constitution. Members of Congress have power to make all laws that they deem necessary for the welfare of the nation. Each of the fifty states has its own state constitution and has a state legislature to make laws for the people residing in that state. The United States Constitution places certain prohibitions on the states, mainly to prevent them from passing laws that are the business of the national government. Congress:

- Makes laws in the United States.

- Can declare war. The President may recommend war, but only Congress can declare war.

- Makes laws for the naturalization of foreigners.

- Establishes and partially controls post offices.

- Establishes courts.

- Coins money.

- Grants patents and copyrights.

- Raises money for government expenses by taxing products imported from other countries and certain products manufactured at home.

- Exercises some authority over the District of Columbia.

Prohibitions on Congress

The Constitution prohibits Congress from doing certain things. Congress:

- Cannot tax products exported from the United States.

- Cannot grant titles of nobility.

- Cannot spend money in the United States except as prescribed by law.

- Cannot pass trade laws that do not deal with states in an equal manner.

- Cannot suspend the writ of **habeas corpus**, meaning that they cannot imprison a person without a trial, except during wartime.

- Cannot pass an **ex post facto law**. An ex post facto law is a law that changes the penalty after an offense has been committed, or makes punishable an offense that was not punishable when committed.

- Cannot pass a **bill of attainder**, a measure that inflicts punishment without a judicial trial.

How a Bill Becomes a Law

The main duty of Congress is to make laws in the United States. All laws made in the United States must correspond with the principles of the Constitution. Laws are made by both houses of Congress working together, with presidential consent. Orders and resolutions that require the concurrence of both houses must also be sent to the President for his signature or veto. Neither the Senate nor the House of Representatives can make laws alone.

A proposed law is called a bill. There are three ways that bills may become laws:

1. A bill may pass both houses of Congress by a majority vote. It can then be sent to the President. If the President signs the bill, it becomes a law.

2. A bill may pass both houses of Congress by a majority vote and be sent to the President. If the President vetoes, or rejects, the bill, he sends it back to the house of Congress in which the bill started. If both houses pass it again by a two-thirds majority vote, it becomes a law without the President's signature.

3. A bill may pass both houses by a majority vote and be sent to the President. If the President keeps it ten days without signing

or vetoing the bill, it becomes a law without his signature, unless Congress adjourns before the ten days are up.

Congress meets in Washington, D.C., beginning on the 3rd day of January of each year. It usually remains in session until it completes its business for the year. The President may call a special session when he deems it necessary. Several Presidents have called special sessions of Congress. Congress sometimes passes laws that are needed for a short time only, and sometimes passes laws that have unsatisfactory, undesired results. The Constitution provides that all laws passed by Congress may be repealed or changed. That way, the laws that Congress passes adequately reflect the nation's needs.

From the USCIS Sample Questions

Question: What is Congress?
Answer: The Senate and the House of Representatives.

Question: Who elects Congress?
Answer: The people.

Question: Who makes the laws in the United States?
Answer: Congress.

Question: What are the duties of Congress?
Answer: To make laws.

Question: Who has the power to declare war?
Answer: Congress.

For Further Study

Question: All laws in the United States correspond with what?
Answer: With the principles of the Constitution.

Question: Can United States laws be changed?
Answer: Yes.

Question: Name one of the important powers of Congress.
Answer: Make laws; declare war; establish and partially control post offices; establish courts; make laws for the naturalization of foreigners; coin money; grant patents and copyrights; raise money for national expenses.

Question: Name one thing that Congress is prohibited from doing.
Answer: Cannot tax exports; cannot grant titles of nobility; cannot spend money, except as prescribed by law; cannot pass trade laws that treat states differently; cannot suspend the writ of habeas corpus, except in wartime; cannot pass an ex post facto law; cannot pass a bill of attainder.

Question: Name one way that a bill can become law.
Answer: There are three ways: 1. By a majority vote of both houses of Congress and the signature of the President. 2. By a two-thirds majority vote of both houses of Congress over the President's veto. 3. If the President keeps the bill ten days without taking action.

The Senate

Election of the Senate

The Senate is one of the two houses of Congress. There are 100 Senators in Congress; this is because there are two Senators from each state. You should know the names of your state's two Senators. For example, the two Senators in the state of California are Barbara Boxer and Dianne Feinstein.

We elect each Senator for six years; there is no limit to how many times a Senator may be re-elected. In fact, there is no limit to how many times any member of Congress can be re-elected. Every two years, one-third of the Senators shift out of office; that way, the majority of Senators serving at any given time have experience. Unlike members of the House of Representatives, who represent their individual districts, Senators represent their states as a whole. Senators must be at least 30 years old to be eligible for office. They may reside in any part of the state that they represent.

The Vice-President of the United States presides over the Senate and is called the President of the Senate. The President Pro Tempore, or President Pro Tem, presides over the Senate when the Vice-President is absent. The Vice-President can vote only in case of a tie in the Senate. For example, if fifty Senators voted for a bill and fifty voted against it, the Vice-President would cast the deciding vote. Being a member of the Senate, the President Pro Tem may vote on all questions, whether he is presiding or not.

Powers of the Senate

In addition to the general powers given to Congress, the Senate and the House of Representatives have separate powers. The Senate must give consent to many important presidential appointments, including members of the Cabinet and judges of all United States courts. The Senate must also approve presidential appointments of ambassadors and consuls to foreign countries. **Ambassadors** represent our government in diplomatic relations with the governments of other countries. **Consuls** protect American citizens and promote the interests of American trade in foreign countries. Moreover, the Senate must approve all treaties with foreign countries made by the President. Additionally, the Senate can elect a Vice-President if the Electoral College fails to elect one.

In the case of the federal officers, the House of Representatives impeaches and the Senate tries the cases, with the Chief Justice of the Supreme Court presiding over the Senate. **Impeachment** means officially accusing an officer of wrongdoing. The Constitution provides that certain federal officers may be impeached. Among them are the President, Vice-President, and federal judges. If an impeached officer is found guilty, he is removed from office and can never hold office again. If he has committed a crime, he may be tried in the regular courts. In the history of the United States, there have only been two Presidents who have been impeached—Andrew Johnson and Bill Clinton—although they were both **acquitted,** or found innocent. Richard Nixon was almost impeached, but instead chose to resign from office before it could occur.

From the USCIS Sample Questions

Question: How many Senators are there in Congress?
Answer: 100.

Question: Why are there 100 Senators in the United States Senate?
Answer: Two from each state.

Question: Can you name the two Senators from your state?
Answer: _____
In California, the two Senators are Barbara Boxer and Dianne Feinstein.

Question: For how long do we elect each Senator?
Answer: Six years.

Question: How many times may a Senator be re-elected?
Answer: There is no limit.

Question: How many times may a Congressman be re-elected?
Answer: There is no limit.

For Further Study

Question: Who presides over the Senate?
Answer: The Vice-President presides over the Senate.

Question: What powers does the Senate have that the House of Representatives does not?
Answer: The President must have the consent of the Senate when he appoints Cabinet officers, judges of United States courts, and ambassadors and consuls to foreign countries; the President must have the consent of the Senate when he makes treaties; the Senate tries cases of impeachment; the Senate has the power to elect a Vice-President of the United States if the Electoral College fails to elect one.

Question: Who presides over the Senate when the President is tried?
Answer: The Chief Justice of the United States Supreme Court.

LESSON 16

The House of Representatives

Election of the House of Representatives

The House of Representatives is the other house of Congress. The number of representatives in a state depends upon the population of the state. Each state is entitled to at least one representative, no matter how small its population. Each state is divided into Congressional districts. The basis of representation changes every ten years to reflect the most recent United States census data. The House of Representatives now has 435 members, plus one Resident Commissioner from Puerto Rico and one delegate each from American Samoa, the District of Columbia, Guam, and the Virgin Islands. The Resident Commissioner and delegates cannot vote on bills, but they can take part in discussions, vote in committees on which they serve, and request the House to consider issues that are of interest to their constituents.

The Representatives' primary role is to speak for the interests of the people who live in the district in which they are elected. A Representative should be a resident of the district that he represents. A Representative must be at least twenty-five years old. A representative serves two years. There are no limits on the number of terms that a Representative can serve.

The presiding officer of the House of Representatives is called the Speaker of the House. The Speaker is elected by his fellow members. Because the Speaker is one of the Representatives, he can vote on all matters. If both President and Vice-President are unable to serve, the Speaker of the House becomes the President of the United States.

Powers of the House of Representatives

The House of Representatives has several powers that the Senate does not have. The House of Representatives has the power to initiate all bills for raising revenue. As the role of the House of Representatives is to act for the people directly, it makes sense that the power of starting tax measures be given to them. The Senate must vote on all bills for raising revenue, as it does on other bills, but it does not initiate bills for raising revenue. In impeachment situations, the House of Representatives impeaches, while the Senate tries the cases. In elections, the House of Representatives may elect a President of the United States if the Electoral College fails to elect one.

From the USCIS Sample Questions

Question: How many Representatives are there in Congress?
Answer: 435.

Question: For how long do we elect the Representatives?
Answer: Two years.

Question: Who becomes President of the United States if the President and the Vice-President should die?
Answer: Speaker of the House of Representatives.

For Further Study

Question: Who presides over the House of Representatives?
Answer: The Speaker of the House.

Question: What powers does the House of Representatives have that the Senate does not?
Answer: The House of Representatives originates all bills for raising revenue; it impeaches United States officers; it elects a President of the United States if the Electoral College fails to elect one.

The Supreme Court

The Supreme Court

The judicial branch of the United States government includes all federal courts, including the Supreme Court, the highest court in the United States. United States courts are called federal courts. The Constitution established the United States Supreme Court and gave Congress power to establish any other courts that might be found necessary.

The main duty of the Supreme Court is to interpret laws. It consists of nine judges, appointed by the President with the consent of the Senate. The head judge is called the Chief Justice, and the others are Associate Justices. They serve life terms, so that they may be independent from popular opinion and changing politics when they make their decisions. Justice William Rehnquist is the current Chief Justice. Here are the names of the Justices, in order of their entrance into the Supreme Court:

William H. Rehnquist	Chief Justice
John Paul Stevens	Associate Justice
Sandra Day O'Connor	Associate Justice
Antonin Scalia	Associate Justice
Anthony M. Kennedy	Associate Justice
David H. Souter	Associate Justice
Clarence Thomas	Associate Justice
Ruth Bader Ginsburg	Associate Justice
Stephen G. Breyer	Associate Justice

The Supreme Court meets in the Supreme Court building in Washington, D.C. It tries only the most important cases, including all cases involving the United States Constitution. If there is a question as to whether some law agrees with the principles of the Constitution, the Supreme Court will decide the matter. Cases that reach the Supreme Court are often appealed from the appellate courts.

Other Federal Courts

In addition to the Supreme Court, Congress has established several other types of courts, including Circuit Courts of Appeal and District Courts. The number of courts increases with the growth of population. The District Courts try such cases as post office or postal offenses and cases involving United States soldiers and sailors. If the cases are not settled in the District Courts, they may go to the Circuit Court of Appeals. In addition, there are special courts, including the U.S. Court of Claims, the U.S. Court of Customs and Patent Appeals, and Territorial Courts.

Federal Courts

    Supreme Court

    Other Courts

        Circuit Courts of Appeal

        District Courts

    Special Courts

        Court of Claims

        Court of Customs and Patent Appeals

        Territorial Courts

From the USCIS Sample Questions

Question: What is the highest court in the United States?
Answer: The Supreme Court.

Question: What are the duties of the Supreme Court?
Answer: To interpret laws.

Question: How many Supreme Court justices are there?
Answer: Nine (9).

Question: Who selects the Supreme Court justices?
Answer: Appointed by the President.

Question: Who is the Chief Justice of the Supreme Court?
Answer: William Rehnquist.

For Further Study

Question: How is the Supreme Court composed?
Answer: The Supreme Court consists of nine members: one Chief Justice and eight Associate Justices.

Question: Who must approve the President's Supreme Court Justice appointments?
Answer: The Senate.

Question: Who are the Associate Justices of the United States Supreme Court?
Answer: The Associate Justices are John Paul Stevens, Sandra Day O'Connor, Antonin Scalia, Anthony M. Kennedy, David H. Souter, Clarence Thomas, Ruth Bader Ginsburg, and Stephen G. Breyer.

LESSON 18

State Executive Branch

The head executive of the state government is the Governor. The powers and duties of the Governor on a state level are similar to those of the President of the United States on a federal level. The Governor oversees law enforcement; signs and vetoes bills; appoints officers and boards; grants pardons, reprieves, and commutations; calls special sessions of the legislature; and is Commander-in-Chief of the state militia. In most states, the Governor appoints a group like the President's Cabinet that assists in making important state decisions.

A state's Lieutenant Governor is much like the Vice-President of the United States. The Lieutenant Governor presides over the State Senate, and takes the place of the Governor whenever necessary. Voters elect both the Governor and Lieutenant Governor of a state; however, the Lieutenant Governor is elected independently of the Governor, so the two executive leaders of a state do not necessarily belong to the same political party. In many states, state officers are elected for four-year terms, although some states hold elections for these positions every two years.

The executive branch of state government also includes a variety of appointed and elected individuals that help manage state affairs. Other state officers usually elected by the people include: Secretary of State, State Treasurer, Attorney General, State Controller or Auditor, and State Superintendent of Schools. There are also various boards, commissions, and departments with specialized powers and functions. The Governor usually appoints members of these groups, but sometimes the voters elect them. Typical state boards or commissions are: Board of Health, Board of Education, Board of Prison Directors, State Tax Commission, Department of Social Welfare, Department of Finance, State Aeronautics Commission, and Personnel Board.

From the USCIS Sample Questions

Question: What is the head executive of a state government called?
Answer: Governor.

For Further Study

Question: What state officer corresponds to the President?
Answer: The Governor.

Question: What state officer corresponds to the Vice-President?
Answer: The Lieutenant Governor.

Question: Name some other state officers who are usually elected.
Answer: The Secretary of State, State Treasurer, Attorney General, State Controller or Auditor, and State Superintendent of Schools.

State Legislative Branch

The State Legislature

The United States Constitution is the supreme law of the United States; similarly, each of the fifty states has its own constitution that is the supreme law of that particular state. The only restriction on state constitutions is that they must not conflict with the United States Constitution.

The law-making or legislative branch of the state government is usually called a state legislature. It is divided into two groups or houses, called a **bicameral** legislature. The upper house is called the State Senate; State Senators are usually elected for four-year terms. The members of the lower house, the State House of Representatives or State Assembly, usually serve two-year terms. Nebraska is one exception; it has a **unicameral** legislature, which means there is only one legislative house.

Law-Making in the States

The legislative process for state governments is similar to that of Congress and the federal government. Any legislator who wants to make a new law presents a document, known as a **bill**, to the house to which he belongs. If a majority in each house approves the bill, the Governor must approve or veto the measure. If the Governor vetoes or refuses to sign the bill, it will not become a state law unless the legislators vote on the bill again. In most cases, the bill must receive approval from a two-thirds majority vote of the members of both houses of the legislature in order to create a law.

For Further Study

Question: What is the legislative branch of the state?
Answer: The legislative branch of the state is the state legislature.

Question: What are the divisions of the state legislatures?
Answer: Most state legislatures have two houses: 1. the State Senate and 2. the State Assembly or State House of Representatives.

Question: Can a Governor veto a bill from the state legislature like the President can veto a bill from Congress?
Answer: Yes.

LESSON 20

State Judicial Branch

The State Supreme Court

The judicial branch of a state includes state courts, county courts, city courts, village courts, and township courts. The highest court is the State Supreme Court, which usually consists of seven judges: a Chief Justice and six Associate Justices. Unlike the federal Supreme Court Justices, voters elect State Supreme Court Justices. The Court tries the most important cases in the state, including all cases pertaining to the state constitution. The State Supreme Court also tries certain cases that have been appealed from the lower courts.

Other State Courts

Below the State Supreme Court are the Courts of Appeal. These courts are principally concerned with appeals from the Superior Courts. Each county in the state has a Superior Court with elected judges. The Superior Court tries most of the common cases, except very small cases that may be settled in the lower courts. Among the cases frequently tried in the Superior Court are: divorces; cases involving land, money, or other property; burglary; embezzlement; murder; and serious assault.

Cities may also have Municipal or Justice Courts. In these courts, minor cases—such as disorderly conduct, drunkenness, vagrancy, automobile speeding, breaking of local ordinances, and small property cases—are tried and settled. Preliminary trials for more serious offenses—like murder or burglary—are also held in local courts. If the evidence warrants, the accused person is then sent to trial in the Superior Court, and is either released on bail or imprisoned in the county jail until his trial takes place.

Every part of the United States is within some court's jurisdiction. The judicial branch of our government extends its protection to all. Small courts deal with minor local issues, while larger courts handle more important cases. At the top of this hierarchy, the State Supreme Court hears the most significant cases, including those that question the constitutionality of state laws. On a national level, the federal Supreme Court serves as the ultimate authority.

For Further Study

Question: What is the judicial branch of the state?
Answer: The judicial branch includes all state courts.

Question: How do the judges of the State Supreme Court secure their positions?
Answer: Voters select the judges of the State Supreme Court in statewide elections.

State Example: California

California History

California is geographically the third largest state in the United States. California was initially a Spanish colony. The first Europeans to enter California were Spanish missionaries. It became part of Mexican territory in 1822. When American immigration began in 1826, some people wanted to be under American rule, while others wanted to be under Mexican control. In 1848, by the terms of a treaty with Mexico, California became part of the United States. In the same year, the discovery of gold prompted widespread immigration from all sections of the United States and from European countries. California officially became a state in 1850. Since then, California has grown steadily and rapidly in population and in prosperity.

California Government

The capital of the state of California is Sacramento. As the political center of the state, Sacramento contains the headquarters of the state's executive, legislative, and judicial leaders.

The head of the executive branch of a state is known as a Governor. Arnold Schwarzenegger is the current Governor of California. The Lieutenant Governor is similar to the Vice-President of the United States, but on a state scale. However, unlike the federal government, the Lieutenant Governor is elected independently of the Governor. Cruz Bustamante is the current Lieutenant Governor of California.

The California legislature consists of two houses called the Senate and the Assembly. They are elected by districts and must reside in the districts that they represent. The term of office of State Senators is four years, and of Assembly members two years. The Lieutenant Governor presides over the State Senate; a Speaker, elected by the assemblymen, presides over the State Assembly. The California Legislature meets in regular sessions each January in

Sacramento. Special sessions can be called by the Governor at any time to consider an important current problem.

There are also state courts that serve as the judicial branch of state governments; the California Superior Court is the highest court that decides California cases.

California Law-Making

If a majority in each house of the state legislature approves a bill, the Governor must approve or veto the measure for it to become a law. If the Governor of California vetoes a bill, it may be passed by a two-thirds majority of both houses of the legislature. If the Governor keeps the bill ten days, it becomes a law unless the ten days are at the end of a session. The Governor has 30 days to sign bills after the end of a session.

An amendment to the California Constitution may be proposed in either house of the legislature. If passed by both houses by a two-thirds majority vote, the amendment is submitted to the people. If a majority of the votes cast are in favor of the amendment, it becomes part of the constitution.

California and several other states have introduced some modern features in legislation. Among these are the initiative, the referendum, and the recall.

- **Initiative:** Laws usually originate in one of the two houses of the legislature. By the initiative system, voters may propose a law via petition. If a sufficient number of voters sign the petition, the proposed law may be placed on the ballot to be voted upon directly by the people.

- **Referendum:** Citizens may circulate petitions if the legislature passes a law that the voters dislike. If a required number of voters sign the petition, the law is deferred, and is placed upon the ballot at the next state election. If a majority of citizens vote against the law at the election, it does not go into effect.

- **Recall:** If citizens are not satisfied with elected public officers, they may circulate petitions calling for an election for their replacements. In 2003, Governor Gray Davis was officially recalled by California voters; actor and businessman Arnold Schwarzenegger received sufficient votes to take over the office of Governor.

The initiative, referendum, and recall are measures that promote greater democracy, since the majority of the voters' wishes prevail in each case. These features take more time, money, and resources than the standard legislative and election process; however, they permit citizens to have an active role in their state government.

From the USCIS Sample Questions

Question: What is the capital of your state?
Answer: _____
The capital of California is Sacramento.

Question: Who is the current Governor of your state?
Answer: _____
Arnold Schwarzenegger is the current Governor of California.

For Further Study

Question: In what city does your state's legislature meet?
Answer: _____
In California, it meets in the capital city of Sacramento.

Question: What is the title of the officer who presides over the Senate in your state?
Answer: _____
In California, the Lieutenant Governor presides over the Senate.

Question: What is the title of the officer who presides over the Assembly in your state?
Answer: _____
In California, the Speaker presides over the Assembly.

Question: What is the term of office of members of the legislature in your state?
Answer: _____
In California, the term of office of State Senators is four years, and of Assembly members is two years.

Question: What is an initiative?
Answer: A method by which laws and some amendments originate with the voters instead of in the legislature, and are voted upon by the people.

Question: What is a referendum?
Answer: A method by which voters determine whether a law passed by the legislature should go into effect.

Question: What is a recall?
Answer: A method by which an unsatisfactory officer may be replaced through a direct election by the voters.

Local Government: County Level

Each state is divided into smaller districts called counties. In each county, there is one town or city that is the headquarters of the county government and is known as the county seat. County governments are usually run by a Board of Supervisors or a Board of County Commissioners. The voters of the county elect the members of the Board, usually for four-year terms. The number of members on most county boards is an odd number, varying from five to eleven people.

In recent years, some larger counties have employed a County Manager or County Administrator, whose duties are similar to those of the manager of a business. This person is usually appointed, paid, and directed by the Board. He attends to the routine duties that are necessary to keep the county government running. County Manager duties may include the right to hire and fire county workers, supervise county purchases, and arrange space for county offices.

The Board serves both executive and legislative roles in county government. County governments usually derive their power and authority from the state constitution, and they carry out state laws within the district under their control. The Board oversees schools, hospital and welfare services, highway construction and maintenance, assessment and collection of taxes, law enforcement, and many other functions. Counties differ from cities, in that cities are smaller incorporated municipalities within counties. City governments are concerned with providing special services—such as police, fire, and health protection—to their local residents.

In addition to the Board, there are certain other county officers who help complete the work of the county government. Some of these people are elected by the voters; others are appointed either by the county board, the state Governor, or the state legislature. Here is a list of some important county officers:

- **County Clerk:** issues marriage licenses and naturalization papers, is in charge of election returns
- **County Treasurer:** receives and distributes county money
- **County Tax Collector:** collects county taxes
- **County Assessor:** assesses property for county taxation purposes
- **County Recorder:** keeps a record of deeds, mortgages, and transfers of property
- **County Auditor:** audits accounts of county officers
- **County Superintendent of Schools:** supervises all schools in the county
- **County Surveyor:** surveys county lines and boundaries
- **County Coroner:** investigates accidental and suspicious deaths
- **Public Administrator:** probates estates when there is no executor or qualified relative
- **District Attorney:** is the county lawyer and represents the county in court cases

Every county has a court of law, usually known as the County Court or Superior Court, located at the courthouse in the county seat. The county runs additional courts called Municipal Courts, Justice Courts, Police Courts, and City Courts in outlying areas of the county. The Superior Court is the judicial branch of county government.

For Further Study

Question: What is the legislative branch of the county government?
Answer: The Board of County Supervisors or County Commissioners.

Question: What is the executive branch of county government?
Answer: The Board of County Supervisors or County Commissioners.

Question: What is the judicial branch of the county government?
Answer: The Superior Court is the judicial branch of the county government.

LESSON 23

County Example: Los Angeles County

Los Angeles County was established in 1850 when California be-came an official state in the Union. Originally an undeveloped area, this county has multiplied in population over the last 150 years. Los Angeles County is now the largest county in the United States. There are almost ten million people living in Los Angeles County, which is 28% of the California population. The county has a diver-sity of ethnicities: Hispanics, Caucasians, Asians, African-Americans, American Indians, and Pacific Islanders have the highest populations, although immigrants have traveled here from nearly every foreign country. 88 cities exist within Los Angeles County, in-cluding the City of Los Angeles, which has almost four million resi-dents.

Because it is so immense and diverse, Los Angeles County gov-ernment must play a large role in supplying services for its inhabi-tants. The County receives money from the federal government, the state of California, and property taxes that are levied on home-own-ers who reside within the county. It uses this revenue to provide many public services to residents. In Los Angeles County, these in-clude supplying county jobs, social and health services, public safety and protection, parks and recreation, environmental conser-vation programs, and cultural opportunities.

The head of Los Angeles County is the Board of Supervisors. There are five supervisors on the Board, who are elected within their districts to serve four-year terms. Unlike leaders at federal and state levels of government, the Board serves as the executive, legislative, and sometimes judicial branch of Los Angeles County. The citizens of the county elect the sheriff, district attorney, and county assessor, but the Board appoints all other leaders in county positions.

For Further Study

Question: What is the name of the governing board of your county?
Answer: _____
In Los Angeles County, it is the Board of Supervisors.

Question: How many members are on the board of your county?
Answer: _____
In Los Angeles County, there are 5 members.

Question: What officials are elected by the voters in your county?
Answer: _____
In Los Angeles County, the members of the Board of Supervisors, the sheriff, the district attorney, and the county assessor.

Local Government: City Level

Like the federal, state, and county governments, the city government has three departments. The head or chief executive of a city is called the Mayor. The legislative branch of a city is usually the City Council or Board of Supervisors. The judicial branch of a city includes municipal courts, which has both Police Courts and Justice Courts. You should be familiar with the names of your local city leaders, especially the head executive—the Mayor—of your city government.

Among the usual city officers are the Treasurer, Tax Collector, Assessor, Auditor, Health Officer, Clerk, Engineer, Police Chief, Fire Chief, and several minor officers. Either the voters elect these officers, or the mayor appoints them. A number of cities have City Administrators, whose duties correspond to those of the County Managers.

The constitution of a city is called a charter. City laws are called ordinances. These ordinances differ by community, in accordance with the wishes of the citizens. Among the well-known ordinances in cities are the automobile regulations, bicycle-riding policies, building ordinances, and health regulations.

Your city government is a very important level of government. Although the federal government handles matters of domestic and international importance and has a great overall effect on the lives of American citizens, individuals living in the United States have limited access to their national leaders. On a local level, however, residents can have considerable access to their representatives. Local ordinances affect many aspects of daily life, and your city government provides services that are fundamental to communities.

One of the essential aspects of local city government is that citizens can influence the way their city runs. You can find out more about your city by attending public meetings, going to City Hall, and meeting your local representatives. You can change things you do not like about your city by letting your representatives know what issues are important to you. It is both a right and responsibility of a citizen to participate and keep your city running smoothly.

From the USCIS Sample Questions

Question: What is the head executive of a city government called?
Answer: Mayor.

For Further Study

Question: What is the legislative branch of a city?
Answer: The City Council or Board of Supervisors.

Question: What is the constitution of a city called?
Answer: A charter.

Question: What are city laws called?
Answer: Ordinances.

LESSON 25

City Example: City of Los Angeles

The City of Los Angeles is the second largest city in the United States, with a population of almost four million people. Not only is Los Angeles highly populated, but it also contains a very high number of immigrants. Many residents of Los Angeles are legal aliens who are preparing to take their naturalization exam to become citizens of the United States.

Los Angeles follows the Mayor-Council system of government. The Mayor of Los Angeles, James Hahn, is the head executive officer of city government. Elected by city residents, the Mayor serves a four-year term in office. Working closely with the City Council, the Mayor enforces laws and ordinances, collaborates with Council members on city issues, and signs or vetoes city ordinances. He also appoints and removes some City officials, submits the annual budget, and represents the City of Los Angeles and its residents in public matters.

The Los Angeles City Council is the head legislative group in the City of Los Angeles. There are 15 members of the Council, each representing one of 15 districts within the City. The Council creates ordinances for approval by the Mayor, approves mayoral appointments, accepts or changes the City budget, imposes taxes, and approves local public developments and services.

The Los Angeles City Charter is essentially the constitution for the local city government. It outlines the rules and regulations that establish Los Angeles city government structure and the roles of city officers. It includes the Mayor as chief executive, the Council as the legislative branch, and numerous departments, bureaus, boards, and commisions that help manage different local matters. Established in 1850 when Los Angeles was incorporated, the City Charter was recently amended. Effective July 1, 2000, the new City Charter has been improved so that the City of Los Angeles can function optimally.

Question: Who is the head of your local government?
Answer: _____
In Los Angeles, the head of local government is Mayor James Hahn.

For Further Study

Question: Who is/are your City Council representative(s)?
Answer: _____
In Los Angeles, there are 15 City Council representatives, each serving a different district:

District 1: Ed Reyes
District 2: Wendy Greuel
District 3: Dennis P. Zine
District 4: Tom LaBonge
District 5: Jack Weiss
District 6: Tony Cardenas
District 7: Alex Padilla
District 8: Bernard Parks
District 9: Jan Perry
District 10: Martin Ludlow
District 11: Cindy Miscikowski
District 12: Greig Smith
District 13: Eric Garcetti
District 14: Antonio Villaraigosa
District 15: Janice Hahn

Question: How many representatives are there in your City Council or Board of Supervisors?
Answer: _____
In Los Angeles, there are 15 members of the City Council.

Suggestions to Teachers

This book presents the essentials of American civics, history, politics, and government. Work in the classroom may be greatly broadened by introducing supplementary material. The following suggestions are indicative of the possibilities. Please feel free to supplement the information presented with whatever materials and opportunities you have. Additionally, please send us ideas so that we can share them with other teachers. Please contact us at:

D.L. Hennessey Publishing
P.O. Box 115
Los Altos, CA 94023
Phone: (800) 355-5129
Fax: (800) 355-5129
E-mail: info@dlhpublishing.com
Website: www.dlhpublishing.com

Introduction to Citizenship

- Discuss why each student wants to become a United States citizen.

- Review Form N-400.

- Invite former students who have taken the naturalization exam. Encourage them to describe their experiences with the citizenship test and process in front of the class.

Lesson 1—The Fifty States

- Display a map of the United States and discuss important landmarks and features.

- Show photographs or videos of natural wonders.

- Have students choose a state (not the one that they live in) and create a report on various aspects of that state (history, government, state bird, state flower, landmarks, etc.).

Lesson 2—American Symbols and Holidays

- Discuss traditions and customs associated with holidays. Discuss other holidays not listed in the lesson, such as Valentine's Day, St. Patrick's Day, and Halloween.
- Sing holiday songs.
- Discuss holiday traditions and customs unique to the students' countries of origin.
- Display American flag in classroom. Compare flag to colonial flag with 13 stars.
- Sing patriotic songs.
- Recite the Pledge of Allegiance.

Lesson 3—Early American History

- Trace Columbus' voyage to the New World on a map.
- Hold a Thanksgiving feast potluck. Have students bring in different types of Thanksgiving food, such as turkey, cranberry sauce, stuffing, and pumpkin pie.

Lesson 4—Revolutionary War

- Study Declaration of Independence. Read document to class and discuss meaning.

Lesson 5—Making of the Constitution

- Discuss differences between Articles of Confederation and the Constitution.

Lesson 6—Constitutional Amendments

- Assign amendments to students and discuss the practical applications.
- Discuss the failure of prohibition and the repealing of the 18th amendment.
- When this nation was founded, although "all men are created equal," not all groups had the right to vote. Discuss all amendments that extended suffrage in the United States.

Lesson 7—History 19th Century

* Assign wars or conflicts to students and have them write a paragraph about one of the leaders or important events.

Lesson 8—History 20th Century

* Assign wars or conflicts to students and have them write a paragraph about one of the leaders or important events.

Lesson 9—Federalism

* Discuss the advantages and disadvantages of federalism, separation of powers, and checks and balances.

Lesson 10—Voting

* Bring in sample ballot and describe the voting process.
* Explain voter registration, including local registration locations and dates of upcoming elections.
* Talk about the main differences between the Republican and Democratic parties.

Lesson 11—Election of the President

* Discuss how the Electoral College elected President George W. Bush over candidate Al Gore, who received the majority of votes, in the November 2000 election.
* Discuss the 2004 presidential election.

Lesson 12—Presidential Powers

* Several Presidents have resigned, been impeached, been assassinated, or have died while in office. Discuss these specific situations and the Vice-Presidents' transition to the presidency.
* Have students write a paragraph or report on a President of their choice and share with the class.

Lesson 13—The President's Cabinet

* The most recent addition to the President's Cabinet is the Office of Homeland Security. Discuss the origin and purposes of this new office, including the role of the USCIS.

Lesson 14—Congressional Powers and Law-Making

• Choose a recently proposed bill and track its progress through Congress.

Lesson 15—The Senate

• Discuss the importance of a bicameral legislature. Include why it is important that Senators represent constituents on a state level.

• Introduce Senators for your state, including pictures, biographies, and political parties.

• Discuss scenarios in history in which impeachment was an issue (Johnson, Nixon, and Clinton).

Lesson 16—The House of Representatives

• Discuss the importance of a bicameral legislature. Include why it is important that Representatives stand for constituents on a district level.

• Introduce the Representative for your district, including a picture, biography, and political party.

• Show a map of your district.

Lesson 17—The Supreme Court

• Bring in current events relating to Supreme Court cases.

• Supreme Court Justices serve life terms. Explain why this is important in terms of political influence.

Lesson 18—State Executive Branch

• Introduce the officers of your state and explain the roles they play in government. Include pictures, biographies, and political parties.

• Examine current issues concerning your state government.

Lesson 19—State Legislative Branch

• Track a bill's progress in your state's legislature.

• Present laws unique to your state.

Lesson 20—State Judicial Branch

• Hold a mock trial.

• Watch part of a trial on Court TV.

Lesson 21—State Example: California

• Using Lesson 21 as an example, present history and government lessons of your state.

• Create a list of advantages of living in your state. Encourage students to share what they like about your state.

Lesson 22—Local Government: County Level

• Attend a trial at your county courthouse.

Lesson 23—County Example: Los Angeles County

• Using Lesson 23 as an example, present history and government lessons of your county.

Lesson 24—Local Government: City Level

• Invite your mayor and other representatives of local government to talk to your class. Have leaders emphasize their own particular duties and functions.

• Visit local City Hall on a field trip.

Lesson 25—City Example: City of Los Angeles

• Using Lesson 25 as an example, present history and government lessons of your city.

APPENDIX B
English Proficiency

In addition to testing your knowledge of United States history and civics, your examiner will also test your ability to read, write, and speak basic English. While your examiner will not expect you to speak perfect English, he wants to ensure that you will be able to clearly communicate and participate in society. If you are not a native English speaker, we highly recommend that you join an English as a Second Language (ESL) class through your local community college or adult education school. These courses will often be free or inexpensive. If you need to work on your English skills, an ESL class is a great place to start. If you speak English but would like to sharpen your speaking skills, look into joining a public speaking organization.

During the citizenship examination, your English skills can be tested in a variety of ways, including any combination of the following:

- General conversation from the moment you begin interacting with the examiner.

- Your ability to answer history and civics questions.

- Your ability to read, write, and speak about the N-400 form (for this reason, you should be very familiar with the form, particularly the "good moral character" questions. Some of these questions may be confusing. See Appendix C for more information).

- Simple civics, history, or everyday life sentences. Below are the sample sentences provided by the USCIS. Actual sentences may vary, but the level of difficulty should remain the same.

The passage below is taken from the USCIS

SAMPLE SENTENCES FOR WRITTEN ENGLISH TESTING

To be eligible for naturalization, you must be able to read, write, and speak basic English. The sentences on this page are **examples** of the types of sentences an USCIS officer may ask you to read aloud or write during your interview. They are not an exhaustive list. **The USCIS officer who interviews you may ask you to read or write other sentences.**

Civics/History

A Senator is elected for 6 years.
_____ is the Vice President of the United States.
All people want to be free.
America is the land of freedom.
All United States citizens have the right to vote.
America is the home of the brave.
America is the land of the free.
_____ is the President of the United States.
Citizens have the right to vote.
Congress is part of the American government.
Congress meets in Washington, D.C.
Congress passes laws in the United States.
George Washington was the first president.
I want to be a citizen of the United States.
I want to be an American citizen.
I want to become an American so I can vote.
It is important for all citizens to vote.
Many people come to America for freedom.
Many people have died for freedom.
Martha Washington was the first "first lady."
Only Congress can declare war.
Our Government is divided into three branches.
People in America have the right to freedom.
People vote for the President in November.
The American flag has stars and stripes.

The American flag has 13 stripes.
The capital of the United States is Washington, D.C.
The colors of the flag are red, white, and blue.
The Constitution is the supreme law of our land.
The flag of the United States has 50 stars.
The House and Senate are parts of Congress.
The people have a voice in Government.
The people in the class took a citizenship test.
The President enforces the laws.
The President has the power of veto.
The President is elected every 4 years.
The President lives in the White House.
The President lives in Washington, D.C.
The President must be an American citizen.
The President must be born in the United States.
The President signs bills into law.
The stars of the American flag are white.
The Statue of Liberty was a gift from France.
The stripes of the American flag are red and white.
The White House is in Washington, D.C.
The United States flag is red, white, and blue.
The United States of America has 50 states.
There are 50 states in the Union.
There are three branches of government.

Everyday Life

He came to live with his brother.
He has a very big dog.
He knows how to ride a bike.
He wanted to find a job.
He wanted to talk to his boss.
He went to the post office.
His wife is at work right now.
His wife worked in the house.
I am too busy to talk today.
I bought a blue car today.
I came to _____ (city) today for my interview.
I count the cars as they pass by the office.

I drive a blue car to work.
I go to work every day.
I have three children.
I know how to speak English.
I live in the State of _____.
I want to be a United States citizen.
It is a good job to start with.
My car does not work.
She can speak English very well.
She cooks for her friends.
She is my daughter, and he is my son.
She needs to buy some new clothes.
She wanted to live near her brother.
She was happy with her house.
The boy threw a ball.
The children bought a newspaper.
The children play at school.
The children wanted a television.
The man wanted to get a job.
The teacher was proud of her class.
The white house has a big tree.
They are a very happy family.
They are very happy with their car.
They buy many things at the store.
They came to live in the United States.
They go to the grocery store.
They have horses on their farm.
They live together in a big house.
They work well together.
Today I am going to the store.
Today is a sunny day.
Warm clothing was on sale in the store.
We are very smart to learn this.
We have a very clean house.
You cook very well.
You drink too much coffee.
You work very hard at your job.

APPENDIX C

Questions from Form N-400

You should be familiar with all aspects of Form N-400, "Application to File Petition for Naturalization." During the oral examination, your examiner will ask you questions from the form to verify that you are being truthful, that you qualify for citizenship, and that you can understand and speak English.

In order to be fully prepared for the examination, you should be familiar with your answers from the form that you submitted. We recommend that you photocopy your completed form before you mail it to the USCIS. This will give you an opportunity to review your answers before your exam. Inform the officer if any of the information has changed since you submitted your form. Additionally, you should be honest and consistent with the examiner.

You should pay particular attention to Section D on "good moral character." Some of these questions may be confusing. Be prepared to discuss what the questions mean. For example, you might be asked Question 22 from Section D: "Have you ever been a habitual drunkard?" If you answer no, the examiner might want to make sure that you understand the question. He might ask you, "What does it mean to be a habitual drunkard?" You should respond with something like: "A habitual drunkard is someone who drinks too much alcohol."

If you have trouble understanding the questions, make sure that you have somebody help you before your examination. If you have any questions or concerns about the N-400 form, you should consider consulting an attorney or immigration lawyer.

APPENDIX D

Patriotic Songs

Star-Spangled Banner

Oh, say! Can you see, by the dawn's early light,
What so proudly we hailed, at the twilight's last gleaming?
Whose broad stripes and bright stars, through the perilous fight,
O'er the ramparts we watched were so gallantly streaming.
And the rockets' red glare, the bombs bursting in air,
Gave proof through the night, that our flag was still there.
Oh, say does the Star-Spangled Banner yet wave
O'er the land of the free and the home of the brave?

America

My country, 'tis of thee. Sweet land of liberty.
    Of thee I sing;
Land where my fathers died!
Land of the Pilgrims' pride!
From every mountain-side
    Let freedom ring.
Our Fathers' God, to Thee, Author of liberty,
    To Thee we sing;
Long may our land be bright
With freedom's holy light;
Protect us by Thy might,
    Great God, our King.

America, the Beautiful

O beautiful for spacious skies,
For amber waves of grain,
For purple mountain majesties
Above the fruited plain!
America! America! God shed His grace on thee
And crown thy good with brotherhood
From sea to shining sea!

O beautiful for patriot dream
That sees beyond the years,
Thine alabaster cities gleam
Undimmed by human tears!
America! America!
God shed His grace on thee
Till nobler men keep once again
Thy whiter jubilee!

APPENDIX E
Oath of Allegiance

"I hereby declare, on oath, that I absolutely and entirely renounce and abjure all allegiance and fidelity to any foreign prince, potentate, state, or sovereignty of whom or which I have heretofore been a subject or citizen; that I will support and defend the Constitution and the laws of the United States of America against all enemies, foreign and domestic; that I will bear true faith and allegiance to the same; that I will bear arms on behalf of the United States when required by law; that I will perform noncombatant service in the Armed Forces of the United States when required by the law; or that I will perform work of national importance under civilian direction when required by the law; and that I take this obligation freely without any mental reservation or purpose of evasion: so help me God. . . ."

APPENDIX F

The Declaration of Independence

In Congress, July 4, 1776
The Unanimous Declaration of the Thirteen United States of America

When in the course of human events, it becomes necessary for one people to dissolve the political bands which have connected them with another, and to assume among the powers of the earth, the separate and equal station to which the laws of Nature and of Nature's God entitle them, a decent respect to the opinions of mankind requires that they should declare the causes which impel them to the separation.

We hold these truths to be self-evident, that all men are created equal, that they are endowed by their Creator with certain inalienable rights, that among these are life, liberty and the pursuit of happiness. That to secure these rights, governments are instituted among men, deriving their just powers from the consent of the governed. That whenever any form of government becomes destructive to these ends, it is the right of the people to alter or to abolish it, and to institute new government, laying its foundation on such principles and organizing its powers in such form, as to them shall seem most likely to affect their safety and happiness. Prudence, indeed, will dictate that governments long established should not be changed for light and transient causes; and accordingly all experience hath shown, that mankind are more disposed to suffer, while evils are sufferable, than to right themselves by abolishing the forms to which they are accustomed. But when a long train of abuses and usurpations, pursuing invariably the same object evinces a design to reduce them under absolute despotism, it is their right, it is their duty, to throw off such government, and to provide new guards for their future security. Such has been the patient sufferance of these

Colonies; and such is now the necessity which constrains them to alter their former systems of government. The history of the present King of Great Britain is a history of repeated injuries and usurpations, all having in direct object the establishment of an absolute tyranny over these States . . .

(Here the Declaration lists the specific complaints of the Colonies against the King of England and concludes as follows:)

WE, THEREFORE, the Representatives of the United States of America, in General Congress Assembled, appealing to the Supreme Judge of the words for the rectitude of our intentions, do, in the name, and by authority of the good people of these Colonies, solemnly publish and declare, That these United Colonies are, and of right ought to be FREE AND INDEPENDENT STATES; that they are absolved from all allegiance to the British Crown, and that all political connection between them and the State of Great Britain, is and ought to be totally dissolved, and that as free and independent States, they have full power to levy war, conclude peace, contract alliances, establish commerce, and to do all other acts and things which independent States may of right do. And for the support of this Declaration, with a firm reliance on the protection of Divine Providence, we mutually pledge to each other our lives, our fortunes and our sacred honor.

Constitutional Amendments

1. (1791) The right to freedom of speech, press, religion, peaceable assembly, and petition to change government.
2. (1791) The right to bear arms (the right to have weapons or own a gun).
3. (1791) The government cannot quarter, or house, soldiers in the people's homes during peacetime without the people's consent.
4. (1791) The government cannot search or take a person's property without a warrant.
5. (1791) A person may not be tried twice for the same crime and does not have to testify against himself.
6. (1791) A person charged with a crime still has some rights, such as the right to a trial and to have a lawyer.
7. (1791) A person has a right to trial by jury in most cases.
8. (1791) The protection against excessive or unreasonable fines or cruel and unusual punishment.
9. (1791) The people have rights other than those mentioned in the Constitution.
10. (1791) Any power not given to the federal government by the Constitution is a power of either the state or the people.
11. (1798) Defines the authority of the United States judicial department in connection with suits against a state.
12. (1804) Describes the presidential election process.
13. (1865) Forbids slavery.
14. (1868) Makes the former slaves citizens, defines citizenship, and fixes the penalty for depriving citizens of their citizenship rights.

15. (1870) Gives former slaves and their descendants the right to vote.

16. (1913) Gives Congress the power to institute income taxes.

17. (1917) Gives the people the right to elect Senators. Formerly, state legislatures formerly elected the Senators.

18. (1919) Establishes national prohibition, which made the selling and distilling of alcoholic beverages illegal.

19. (1920) Grants suffrage—the right to vote—to women.

20. (1933) States that the President is inaugurated on January 20th, Congress meets on January 3rd, the terms of members of Congress shall begin on January 3, and if the President-elect dies before inauguration, the Vice-President becomes President.

21. (1933) Repeals national prohibition.

22. (1951) Says that no President shall be elected for more than two terms.

23. (1961) Allows District of Columbia citizens to vote for President in national elections. DC has 3 electoral votes, but does not have representation in Congress.

24. (1964) Abolishes poll taxes or other voting taxes in elections for President, Vice-President, Senators, or Representatives in Congress.

25. (1967) Covers the problems of succession to the presidency and vice-presidency and disability of the President.

26. (1971) Changes the voting age from 21 to 18 years.

27. (1992) Relates to salary changes for members of Congress.

APPENDIX H

The Gettysburg Address

Delivered by President Abraham Lincoln at the battlefield in Gettysburg, Pennsylvania, November 19, 1863

Four score and seven years ago, our fathers brought forth on this continent a new nation, conceived in liberty and dedicated to the proposition that all men are created equal.

Now we are engaged in a great civil war, testing whether that nation or any nation so conceived and so dedicated can long endure. We are met on a great battlefield of that war. We have come to dedicate a portion of that field, as a final resting-place of those who here gave their lives that that nation might live. It is altogether fitting and proper that we should do this.

But, in a larger sense, we cannot dedicate—we cannot consecrate—we cannot hallow—this ground. The brave men, living and dead, who struggled here, have consecrated it, far above our poor power to add or detract. The world will little note, nor long remember, what we say here, but it can never forget what they did here. It is for us the living, rather, to be dedicated here to the unfinished work which they who fought here have thus far so nobly advanced. It is rather for us to be here dedicated to the great task remaining before us—that from these honored dead we take increased devotion to that cause for which they gave the last full measure of devotion—that we here highly resolve that these dead shall not have died in vain—that this nation, under God, shall have a new birth of freedom—and that government of the people, by the people, for the people shall not perish from the earth.

Presidents of the United States

1. George Washington 1789–1797
2. John Adams 1797–1801
3. Thomas Jefferson 1801–1809
4. James Madison 1809–1817
5. James Monroe 1817–1825
6. John Quincy Adams 1825–1829
7. Andrew Jackson 1829–1837
8. Martin Van Buren 1837–1841
9. William Henry Harrison 1841–1841
10. John Tyler 1841–1845
11. James K. Polk 1845–1849
12. Zachary Taylor 1849–1850
13. Millard Fillmore 1850–1853
14. Franklin Pierce 1853–1857
15. James Buchanan 1857–1861
16. Abraham Lincoln 1861–1865
17. Andrew Johnson 1865–1869
18. Ulysses S. Grant 1869–1877
19. Rutherford B. Hayes 1877–1881
20. James A. Garfield 1881–1881
21. Chester A. Arthur 1881–1885
22. Grover Cleveland 1885–1889
23. Benjamin Harrison 1889–1893
    Grover Cleveland 1893–1897
24. William McKinley 1897–1901
25. Theodore Roosevelt 1901–1909
26. William H. Taft 1909–1913
27. Woodrow Wilson 1913–1921
28. Warren G. Harding 1921–1923
29. Calvin Coolidge 1923–1929

House of Representatives Membership by State

Alabama	7	Montana	1
Alaska	1	Nebraska	3
Arizona	8	Nevada	3
Arkansas	4	New Hampshire	2
California	53	New Jersey	13
Colorado	7	New Mexico	3
Connecticut	5	New York	29
Delaware	1	North Carolina	13
Florida	25	North Dakota	1
Georgia	13	Ohio	18
Hawaii	2	Oklahoma	5
Idaho	2	Oregon	5
Illinois	19	Pennsylvania	19
Indiana	9	Rhode Island	2
Iowa	5	South Carolina	6
Kansas	4	South Dakota	1
Kentucky	6	Tennessee	9
Louisiana	7	Texas	32
Maine	2	Utah	3
Maryland	8	Vermont	1
Massachusetts	10	Virginia	11
Michigan	15	Washington	9
Minnesota	8	West Virginia	3
Mississippi	4	Wisconsin	8
Missouri	9	Wyoming	1

APPENDIX K

USCIS
100 Typical Questions

1. What are the colors of our flag?
2. How many stars are there in our flag?
3. What color are the stars on our flag?
4. What do the stars on the flag mean?
5. How many stripes are there in the flag?
6. What color are the stripes?
7. What do the stripes on the flag mean?
8. How many states are there in the Union?
9. What is the 4th of July?
10. What is the date of Independence Day?
11. Independence from whom?
12. What country did we fight during the Revolutionary War?
13. Who was the first President of the United States?
14. Who is the President of the United States today?
15. Who is the Vice-President of the United States today?
16. Who elects the President of the United States?
17. Who becomes President of the United States if the president should die?
18. For how long do we elect the President?
19. What is the Constitution?
20. Can the Constitution be changed?
21. What do we call a change to the Constitution?
22. How many changes or amendments are there to the Constitution?
23. How many branches are there in our government?
24. What are the three branches of our government?
25. What is the legislative branch of our government?
26. Who makes the laws in the United States?
27. What is Congress?
28. What are the duties of Congress?
29. Who elects Congress?
30. How many Senators are there in Congress?
31. Can you name the two Senators from your state?

32. For how long do we elect each Senator?
33. How many representatives are there in Congress?
34. For how long do we elect the Representatives?
35. What is the executive branch of our government?
36. What is the judiciary branch of our government?
37. What are the duties of the Supreme Court?
38. What is the supreme law of the United States?
39. What is the Bill of Rights?
40. What is the capital of your state?
41. Who is the current Governor of your state?
42. Who becomes President of the U.S.A. if the President and the Vice-President should die?
43. Who is the Chief Justice of the Supreme Court?
44. Can you name the thirteen original states?
45. Who said, "Give me liberty or give me death!"?
46. Which countries were our enemies during World War II?
47. What are the 49th and 50th states of the Union?
48. How many terms can a President serve?
49. Who was Martin Luther King, Jr.?
50. Who is the head of your local government?
51. According to the Constitution, a person must meet certain requirements in order to be eligible to become President. Name one of these requirements.
52. Why are there 100 Senators in the Senate?
53. Who selects the Supreme Court Justices?
54. How many Supreme Court Justices are there?
55. Why did the Pilgrims come to America?
56. What is the head executive of a state government called?
57. What is the head executive of a city government called?
58. What holiday was celebrated for the first time by the American colonists?
59. Who was the main writer of the Declaration of Independence?
60. When was the Declaration of Independence adopted?
61. What is the basic belief of the Declaration of Independence?
62. What is the national anthem of the United States?
63. Who wrote the Star-Spangled Banner?
64. Where does freedom of speech come from?
65. What is the minimum voting age in the United States?
66. Who signs bills into law?
67. What is the highest court in the United States?

68. Who was the President during the Civil War?
69. What did the Emancipation Proclamation do?
70. What special group advises the President?
71. Which President is called the "Father of Our Country"?
72. What Immigration and Naturalization Service form is used to apply to become a naturalized citizen?
73. Who helped the Pilgrims in America?
74. What is the name of the ship that brought the Pilgrims to America?
75. What were the 13 original states of the United States called?
76. Name 3 rights or freedoms guaranteed by the Bill of Rights.
77. Who has the power to declare war?
78. What kind of government does the United States have?
79. Which President freed the slaves?
80. In what year was the Constitution written?
81. What are the first 10 amendments to the Constitution called?
82. Name one purpose of the United Nations.
83. Where does Congress meet?
84. Whose rights are guaranteed by the Constitution and the Bill of Rights?
85. What is the introduction to the Constitution called?
86. Name one benefit of being a citizen of the United States.
87. What is the most important right granted to U.S. citizens?
88. What is the United States capitol?
89. What is the White House?
90. Where is the White House located?
91. What is the name of the President's official home?
92. Name one right guaranteed by the First Amendment.
93. Who is the Commander-in-Chief of the U.S. military?
94. Which President was the first Commander-in-chief of the U.S. military?
95. In what month do we vote for the President?
96. In what month is the new President inaugurated?
97. How many times may a Senator be re-elected?
98. How many times may a Congressman be re-elected?
99. What are the 2 major political parties in the U.S. today?
100. How many states are there in the United States?

Answer sheet

1. Red, white, and blue
2. 50
3. White
4. One for each state in the Union
5. 13
6. Red and white
7. They represent the original 13 states
8. 50
9. Independence Day
10. July 4th
11. England
12. England
13. George Washington
14. George W. Bush
15. Dick Cheney
16. The Electoral College
17. Vice President
18. Four years
19. The supreme law of the land
20. Yes
21. Amendments
22. 27
23. 3
24. Legislative, executive, and judiciary
25. Congress
26. Congress
27. The Senate and the House of Representatives
28. To make laws
29. The people
30. 100
31. _____ (insert local information)
32. 6 years
33. 435
34. 2 years .
35. The President, Cabinet, and departments under the Cabinet members
36. The Supreme Court
37. To interpret laws

38. The Constitution
39. The first 10 amendments of the Constitution
40. _____(insert local information)
41. _____(insert local information)
42. Speaker of the House of Representatives
43. William Rehnquist
44. Connecticut, New Hampshire, New York, New Jersey, Massachusetts, Pennsylvania, Delaware, Virginia, North Carolina, South Carolina, Georgia, Rhode Island, and Maryland
45. Patrick Henry
46. Germany, Italy, and Japan
47. Alaska and Hawaii
48. 2
49. A civil rights leader
50. _____(insert local information)
51. Must be a natural born citizen of the United States; must be at least 35 years old by the time he/she will serve; must have live in the United States for at least 14 years
52. Two (2) from each state
53. Appointed by the President
54. Nine (9)
55. For religious freedom
56. Governor
57. Mayor
58. Thanksgiving
59. Thomas Jefferson
60. July 4, 1776
61. That all men are created equal
62. The Star-Spangled Banner
63. Francis Scott Key
64. The Bill of Rights
65. Eighteen (18)
66. The President
67. The Supreme Court
68. Abraham Lincoln
69. Freed many slaves
70. The Cabinet
71. George Washington

71. George Washington
72. Form N-400, "Application to File Petition for Naturalization"
73. The American Indians (Native Americans)
74. The *Mayflower*
75. Colonies
76.
    1. The right of freedom of speech, press, religion, peaceable assembly and requesting change of government
    2. The right to bear arms (the right to have weapons or own a gun, though subject to certain regulations)
    3. The government may not quarter, or house, soldiers in the people's homes during peacetime without the people's consent
    4. The government may not search or take a person's property without a warrant
    5. A person may not be tried twice for the same crime and does not have to testify against himself
    6. A person charged with a crime still has some rights, such as the right to a trial and to have a lawyer
    7. The right to trial by jury in most cases
    8. Protects people against excessive or unreasonable fines or cruel and unusual punishment
    9. The people have rights other than those mentioned in the Constitution
    10. Any power not given to the federal government by the Constitution is a power of either the state or the people
77. The Congress
78. Republican
79. Abraham Lincoln
80. 1787
81. The Bill of Rights
82. For countries to discuss and try to resolve world problems; to provide economic aid to many countries.
83. In the Capitol in Washington, D.C.
84. Everyone (citizens and non-citizens living in the U.S.)
85. The Preamble
86. Obtain federal government jobs; travel with a U.S. passport; petition for close relatives to come to the U.S. to live
87. The right to vote

88. The place where Congress meets
89. The President's official home
90. Washington, D.C. (1600 Pennsylvania Avenue, NW)
91. The White House
92. Freedom of: speech, press, religion, peaceable assembly, and requesting change of the government
93. The President
94. George Washington
95. November
96. January
97. There is no limit
98. There is no limit
99. Democratic and Republican
100. Fifty